ORGASMS

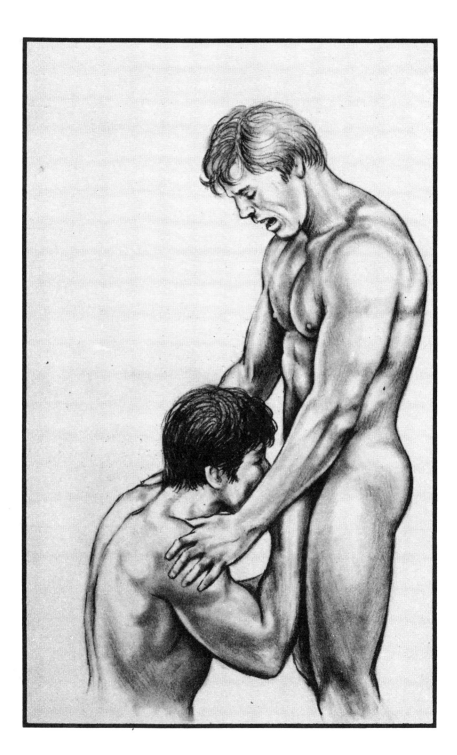

ORGASMS

HOMOSEXUAL ENCOUNTERS
FROM *FIRST HAND*

Volume 2

Edited by
Winston Leyland

Gay Sunshine Press
San Francisco

Cover photo by Kristen Bjorn. Cover design by Timothy Lewis.

Photos © 1985 by Old Reliable (pp. 17, 36, 52, 66, 102, 125)
Photos by Force 1 (pp. 89, 148)
Drawings © 1985 by Tom of Finland (pp. 27, 112, 136, 167)

ISBN 0-917342-12-7

All photos in this book are posed by professional models. The fact that these models are shown does not imply that they are necessarily homosexual, nor that they endorse this book or any particular code of behavior. The stories presented here are true, sexual case histories. The fact that they appear in this book does not mean that the editors or publishers necessarily approve of those acts which may be illegal in some states. It is against the law to have intercourse with boys under 18. But we do print memoirs of men talking about their own boyhood experiences. All stories in this book are true case histories in the tradition of Kinsey and the great sex researchers of this country.

Material published in this book originally appeared in *First Hand Magazine*, P.O. Box 1314, Teaneck, N.J. 07666.

Gay Sunshine Press
P.O. Box 40397
San Francisco, CA 94140
Complete illustrated catalogue of books: $1 ppd.

LA-2001-1-1279

Making It With Ice Cubes

BY   BILL   ANDERSON

E ver wonder what to do with a hot ass? A *really* hot one? Steaming, sizzling, just about to explode? Try ice.

You can get plain or fancy. Tap water in standard cubes for the novice ass-stuffer. Round ice from Perrier water for the health nut. Banana flavored popsicles for the twinky. Absinthe frozen in gigantic cock molds from the sex toy store for those jaded, hard-to-arouse types.

Whatever you use, you'll find a whole new territory of sensation when that frozen liquid hits that flaming asshole and your playmate lets out a yowl of sharp delight. Or, if you're home alone and hot to trot, don't waste those precious cubes on a highball. Break'em out, wash off the sharp edges and shove'em up your chute for one of the cheapest thrills around.

And one of the safest, if you observe a couple of rules even a moron could grasp. First, be sure that whatever your ice is made of, it isn't contaminated. The chances of contracting a disease from frozen water are slight, but why risk it? Water from the tap in a tropical hotel room is out. The general rule is: If you wouldn't drink it, don't put it in an asshole.

Second, melt the rough parts off any frozen object. A fast rinse under tap water will do. Just be sure nothing sharp remains. Otherwise, you could do to the fragile mucous membrane of your ass or somebody else's what that iceberg did to the Titanic. And rectal fissures are no fun.

Beyond that, icestuffing carries one of the fewest risks around. The worst possible scenario would be a possible case of frostbite if you shoved six dozen cubes up there, but by then everything below your waist would be numb. Ice, like ethyl chloride, is a fast-acting sensation. It's almost over before it hits, because the temperature of most rectums (98.6° F.) melts ice within a couple of minutes.

Depending, of course, on how big the piece of ice is.

Some people have been known to experiment with molds that approach the limit of capacity for even the most well-stretched holes. It's not a good idea to get too greedy unless you really *must* show up at your local emergency room with a torn sphincter muscle or a perforated rectum, explaining to the doctor on deck that you iced yourself or somebody else. However, a fast check of the medical literature on reported injuries to the anus or rectum reveals no mention of damage caused by ice. Coke bottles, light bulbs, broomsticks, yes. Ice, no.

The first time I ever experimented with ice was a scene I'll never forget. Nor will the 24-year-old hockey star from Toronto who was in New York for a weekend of fast fun. Blond, built, and obviously ready for rough action, he was perched on the pool table in a bar that never fails to give me what I'm looking for — a twisted mind in a hot body. I let him stare a hole in me for five minutes before I rolled over to introduce myself.

"Hiya, champ. I haven't seen *you* in here before."

"Nah. I live in Toronto, down for a couple of days."

"Wanna get fucked?"

"Sure as hell do."

And we sure as hell did, until those barrel thighs with their light frosting of blond hair were thrashing and pumping and churning like a steam locomotive. And his ass, rock solid, was opening up and clenching down under my ruthless cock. I really poured on the heat. He was gasping.

"Ah, ah, I think I'm gonna shoot! Get some ice!"

"Some what?"

"Ice cubes. I want you to stuff some ice cubes up my ass!"

He was frantic. I think I would have stuffed a watermelon up his ass if he'd asked. His need was great. He rolled over on his back, his massive chest heaving and the ridges of his granite abdominal muscles locking down hard every time he exhaled. The look in his eyes said "Do it!" like a police siren in the night.

So I trotted into the kitchen and broke out the ice cubes. Nothing fancy, just plain water. I didn't know I was going to entertain my guest with ice cubes up the hatch rather than in the usual direction — down.

I padded back into the bedroom with a bowlful of ice cubes. I put two in my mouth and sucked off the corners a little. Then I put my shoulders under the hockey star's incredible thighs and pinned them against his chest. His asshole was thus exposed for maximum attention. With so little body hair, he was presenting a very naked butt for me to work on. And in that position, pinned double on his back, this guy's ass muscles were exposed like huge cables, two deep ridges rounding up into his thighs.

I bent down and began to rim his red hot hole, very slowly at first. But the cubes were melting in my mouth fast, so I used my tongue as a launching pad and pushed both the ice bits into his rosy pucker.

"That's it! That's it!" He was really yelling and pumping his dick like crazy.

"More!"

I grabbed three more cubes, threw them into my mouth and swirled them around frantically. Then I took one cube out and shoved it up his hole, speedily followed by two more. Just to make sure everything was operating right, I pushed my index finger in after them to stir the contents well. A fleeting image of Julia Child, attacking a bowl of batter with her customary hearty gusto, passed through my mind.

"I'm gonna shoot!"

"Want some more ice cubes?"

"Yeah! Yeah! Two more, three more!"

And in they went. I could hear a muffled clink as things began to get a little cozy in that overheated furnace. Hockey star's legs went rigid with anticipation of the load, as he was soon to blow all over both of us.

And then he came. In big, ropy squeezes, like icing on a cake. A gob of it landed right across his chest. Part of it hit his chin, and he slurped that up instantly, eyes rolled to heaven.

"Unh. That was great."

"Yeah, I'll say. How long have you, uh, been into ice," I asked. Immediately I realized I should have put it the other way around.

"I dunno. It must be the hockey. Every kid in Canada gets handed a hockey stick before he can walk, like Southern boys get handed footballs. It's a rough game. You know, all that aggression. Fights. I've been hit all over. And, even as kids, you know, there's all this stuff about 'Up yours' and 'Take it up the ass.' I guess I just made a different connection than some of the other guys. When you take a spill, it's called 'Ice up the ass.'" He smiled agreeably.

From that moment on, it was only a question of time before I would try asshole freezing on the next willing partner. And there have been plenty. I *haunt* the ice cream freezer at my nearby supermarket, hoping for a new marketing stunt to show up in a new flavor or a new shape. For a while, there was boysenberry marmalade ice cream on a stick, molded in the shape of a fair-sized Santa Claus. But it didn't go over. Then there was the all-week frozen banana. I bought every single one in stock. It was a terrific idea for hungry assholes, but apparently the buying public thought otherwise. I never saw them again.

The best answer, though, turned out to be the plastic molds of thick dicks available at the Pleasure Chest, a sex toy store with outlets in New York, Los Angeles and San Francisco (at last count). But you can find these molds almost anywhere. Or, with a little patience and some plaster of Paris, make your own. The only problem with the homemade mold is that it has to fit tightly together in two parts, with a channel left for pouring in liquid. Better stick with the store bought variety. They're reasonably priced.

With the right mold, you're on your own with liquids. I've used coffee, wine (*always* diluted one part wine, five parts water), lemonade. For the perfectionist, a high technique demands that only distilled water will do, first boiled to remove any gases (such as oxygen), so that the finished frozen product will be *solid* water. Otherwise, you might expose tiny bubble pockets in melting that *could* scrape microscopic scars on the anal sphincter muscle or, worse, on the rectal wall itself.

Beyond molds and ready-mades lies a vast frontier where only the truly adventurous dare tread — or sit. Here, the ice sculptor is king. Starting with a 100-pound block of solid ice and a special ice-carving knife, certain highly paid (usually Japanese, sometimes Swiss) chefs can, within a few minutes, find a swan or a bear hidden beneath the surface. Or a phallic image of whatever size and configuration your heart desires. But unless you want to spend a lot of time lurking outside the staff entrance of your local Benihana restaurant, it's best to leave this alone. A plain raspberry popsicle is usually enough to satisfy any but the most perverse craving for that sudden hot lick that only ice imparts to the aroused asshole.

I can hear the crackle of an upended ice tray under running water now. You can't wait to try it. Good. Have an ice day!

Name: Gary   **Age: 27**
San Francisco

I remember my first sexual feelings quite vividly. I was nine years old, sitting in my living room, watching *The Walt Disney Show* on television. The episode featured hunky young men fighting the British during the American Revolution. When one of these hot young men was captured by the British and they wanted information from him, they ripped his shirt off, tied him to a column and began to whip him. As they did, they kept asking him questions which he refused to answer.

On screen, I saw the whip strike his bare back and his muscles tense and convulse as the lash came down. I suddenly felt hot up and down my body and couldn't understand why. I started rubbing my body against a big, thick overstuffed chair in the living room, feeling all kinds of pleasurable sensations rushing through me.

Looking back now, I feel this was the first time I came, although I didn't shoot any semen. All I knew then was that I had felt something strange and wonderful, but was a bit shaken by this discovery.

The following years were characterized by repressed sexual feelings and success at school (although I'm not saying there was necessarily a direct correlation between the two). Eventually, my horniness won out and I had my first wet dream. I awoke from this hazy dream – something about a big, strong guy pinning me down – with my abdomen covered by a sticky, whitish substance. I felt ashamed, thinking I had wet myself. But then I felt the liquid in my fingers and it felt too thick to be urine. I still wanted to wash it off so I crept into the bathroom. When I entered the bathroom, my older brother was standing in the shower with his back to me. Through the translucent shower curtain, I saw his strong back and hairy, muscular legs. As I surreptitiously wiped the cum away from my stomach, thighs, balls and cock head, I wondered if my body would look like my brother's in a few years. My body was changing already, with hairs appearing at the base of my cock and around my balls.

When I returned to bed, I started to play with myself. I felt a surging feeling come into my cock and watched as it hardened and extended. I felt my balls tighten at the base of my cock and watched as the head of my cock throbbed. I took some spit from my mouth and began to rub it along the base of my cock up to the head, stroking myself. I continued to stroke my shaft with my right hand, using the spit as lubricant. Simultaneously, I cupped my balls in my left hand and held them up closer to the base of my cock. I stared at my cock as a big vein that ran diagonally from its base on the left up to the right of the upper shaft thickened and pulsed. I kept stroking the shaft and gripping and rubbing my balls tightly until I shot my load up onto my abdomen, splashing a trail of come up toward my left tit.

I felt relieved and excited at the same time. Quickly, I took the tissues I had brought from the bathroom and wiped myself off. Then, I threw the tissues in my wastebasket, concealing them under some discarded pages from my looseleaf. I had just discovered the joy of masturbation. It felt good and I proceeded to engage in it every couple of nights, while everyone else in my family was asleep.

As I masturbated, I developed my fantasy life. I fantasized myself once as Superman engaged in a wrestling match with Doc Savage, the Man of Bronze. Our bodies struggled against each other, muscle to muscle. We fell to the dirt and began to grip each other's cocks as our mouths opened to each other and our tongues caressed.

At another time, I fantasized letting a big, strong repairman into my house who wound up throwing me against the kitchen table. He pressed my chest against the top of the table. Lying across my back, he pulled my pants down with one strong hand. Then he pressed his cock head in against my asshole and pounded at it until he came and I came. These and other fantasies made up my masturbatory repertoire.

Masturbation was finally enhanced by actual sexual experience in my freshman year of college when I first slept with a woman. We were known by people who roomed near us on college retreats as the loudest couple they'd ever heard. We would moan and scream in our lovemaking. We had fun. One time, we had a baseball game playing on the radio while we were fucking in my parents' apartment. They were at the game and we wanted to know when they'd be heading back. We felt *our* athletics were being commented on as the radio announcer called out, "Ball one! Ball two! It's a hit! Home run!"

At least we kept from getting caught by my parents.

I wasn't always that lucky as time went on. Once when I had a male lover over and we were sharing a shower, my parents came home unexpectedly. I quickly threw on my clothes while my friend dried himself off with a towel. Nobody was really fooled.

But, that's getting ahead of myself. The first time I slept with a man was very warm and intensely felt. A friend of mine confided his love for a man who had just left for the Peace Corps. As he talked about this feeling, he started to cry and I began to comfort him, to hold him. He led me to the bedroom and turned off the light. The next thing I knew he was applying some sort of hair pomade to my cock and his ass. He eased my cock in and I fucked him slowly for a long time. Finally, I increased my tempo and shot my cum into his ass as he stroked his cock until he came.

I remember thinking that "The earth hadn't opened up under my feet. The sky hadn't let loose a lightning bolt to strike me," so what we had done was OK. It was actually more than that; it was wonderful.

The first time I went down on a man occurred with my first lover, a hairy Jewish intellectual type. I sucked his cock so well he asked me if I hadn't done it before. I felt proud about his comment. Another time he told me I was 'well-hung' — a comment which both surprised and embarrassed me. Since he was only the second man I'd been to bed with, I was still assuming that all men's cocks were about the same size. How wrong I was.

With another boyfriend, somewhat later, we both tried fucking each other. It was uncomfortable for both of us so we gave up on it. Still later, a man who became my lover for six years successfully and pleasurably fucked me on a sofa in a friend's apartment, using only butter. After success with butter, he and I went on to other lubricants and both enjoyed fucking and being fucked. We also fucked everywhere from an abandoned World's Fair pavilion to a tiny bathroom at a Fire Island hotel while people pounded on the door to use the facility.

Since he and I ended our love relationship, I have explored other sexual fantasies — especially S&M. In L.A., I once stayed with a friend of a friend who was a topman in S&M sex. I was hot for him but he ignored me sexually until one night when I was asleep and he climbed into my bed and pinned me down. As he pulled his cock out of his black leather pants, he told me he was going to fuck the shit out of me.

He grinned and held me down until I begged him not to do it. Then he just left the room. I felt horny, but was confused by it.

Years later, though, I met a man with whom I've explored my S&M fantasies. One time, he and I went to this dungeon equipped with slings, examining tables, manacles, and T-bars to which people could be bound. He placed me in a sling with my hands and feet bound in stirrups and played with my cock until it was hard and pulsing. Then he grabbed a handful of Crisco from a container that the management had conveniently placed nearby, smoothed it over his cock and into my ass. He positioned his body so that he could thrust his cock deeply into my ass. He kept plugging at me while another man grabbed my cock and pulled at it. I finally came, shooting a large load onto the black wall of the dungeon. Men all around had grabbed their own cocks and were jerking off while watching me. It was truly a scene.

Another scene took place when this same topman took me and bound my wrists and feet to a T-bar. As I was hanging there, he took out a small whip and lashed my back. My back muscles tensed with each stroke of the whip. I had gone full circle from my earliest sexual experience watching a man being whipped to actually being that man. My fantasy had come to life.

Right now, I am involved in both "vanilla" — conventional lovemaking — with my partner, as well as exploring the wilder side of sex (particularly S&M). I enjoy both and would never categorically exclude either from my life. Many of my fantasies are still to be explored. I want to enjoy those fantasies while exploring my deepest emotions with my present partner. I've learned that, for me, trust is the best aphrodisiac. With trust, I can allow myself to experience nearly anything sexually, and I fully intend to do so.

come out to my best friend, and I had no homosexual experiences except in my head. Bob kissed me on the mouth playfully at a wild party, but that didn't count. I never made it with that jock I'd been wild about, and never even found out what his bedtime tastes were.

My sex life turned around 180 degrees when I got out of college and moved to Manhattan. Now it was Bob who had to listen to my sexual adventures. I'll never forget the night I went to see a double-bill at a cheap movie theatre in the East Village. A good looking guy sat down next to me and started playing with my zipper. It was what I'd been waiting nearly a decade for, and it had happened without my even trying. But I was so nervous that the fellow grabbed a handful of limp penis and got up and left.

The next time I did better. It was at a well-known gay movie theatre uptown. I was so engrossed in the hot all-male sex film, that when a guy sat down next to me I almost moved away in irritation. Then I thought, "This is what I came here for!" He unzipped my trousers and sucked my cock while I tried to decide whether I liked it. It felt strange. I was nervous because it was in a public place, although everyone else was much too busy to watch us. I had a tingling thrill up and down my cock, and knew that I had finally pointed myself in the right direction. The man's lips and tongue worked along my shaft. I sighed contentedly, aching to climax. I shot my load in his mouth, and got up, feeling like I'd finally ascended a tricky mountain peak. I wanted more.

My cock was sucked by dozens of faceless strangers in the gay movie houses of Manhattan. I loved it more each time, but I still resisted going down on any other fellow, till finally, one night, I was forced to confront my hang-ups.

My first night in a gay bar I went home with an attractive man in his late thirties: slender, European, very experienced. I was twenty-one. I had been entirely submissive and passive up to that point, sitting back and letting guys suck me without ever returning the favor. That night I was introduced to the other side.

We got undressed. I sat on the side of the bed. Suddenly there was this prick flapping in my face. I knew what he wanted. That first time was not a turn-on for me at all. Afterwards, I was flopped face down on the bed, and he entered my rectum, groaning and sweating, in love with my firm, rounded ass. I felt part rapture, part revulsion. He was too much into the "slam-bam" technique of straight guys, but he initiated me into every basic kind of gay sex that night, and for that I'm grateful.

I cruised at least three nights a week, investigating every bar in New York, including the leather bars down by the docks, the East side conversation and piano lounges, the "wrinkle rooms" (though some of the most vital and the sexiest men are middle-aged or older), discos, and Times Square hustler bars. I hustled on and off for more than two years, cruising when I took time off, becoming adept at sucking cock and fucking and being fucked.

I met my first lover at a bar on the Upper West Side. He was too possessive, so the relationship did not last. He was also more sexually one-sided than I had ever been. I was always forced into the "passive" role — when I really would have preferred fucking and being serviced. I wouldn't have minded it if we both could have been more versatile, but sex with him was limiting and unsatisfying. Maybe our relationship wasn't such a deep one, or sex could have been better resolved between us.

For me there's no greater satisfaction than fucking someone who loves to be fucked. Manly flesh gripping manly flesh, my cock inserted into a tight, but yielding aperture, my lips on his neck, my hands kneading the muscles of his shoulders, his body writhing ecstatically beneath mine. My cock swelled to the largest possible proportion, my head aflame with sensuous thoughts, sounds and smells.

My cock starts slowly, then picks up speed, as I plunge with everquickening thrusts into his body, and his body pushes up in unison with mine. Harder and faster I go, my head spinning, his sighs increasing in volume, his body squirming with unbridled delight, and my whole being concentrating on one thing only: my cock in his ass. I come inside him, he absorbs my passion and we collapse together in a joyous union.

One of my most exciting experiences was my first time in the orgy room of a back room bar. I fucked one guy bent over before me, while another man kissed me, and still another unbuttoned my shirt and wrapped his lips to my nipples. Someone behind me wrapped his arms around my chest and started to fuck me. My pants were lying about my ankles, and there was an air of abandonment to the whole thing that made me feel like one part of a mathematically precise sexual engine. I think each person should try an orgy room at least a dozen times.

I have a lover now and am more "domestic" than ever. It is a deep, strong, emotional relationship of mutual concern and caring. It is also an open relationship; as much as we enjoy sex with each other, we also still enjoy sex with other people. There is no guilt, and no recriminations. Just love for each other, and sexual satisfaction with many.

Name: Tom Age: 25

*T*he first book I ever bought was an illustrated and abridged version of *Tom Sawyer*. My brother told my mother that I bought it because of the picture of naked boys bathing. They were shown from the back, hardly more than outlines. My brother was right. I was in the first grade at that time, and he was in the third.

On a couple of unsupervised afternoons, my brother, two neighborhood boys, and I went into the basement, stripped and danced around in a circle yipping and chanting, probably some variation of "London Bridge," because I remember falling down and laughing, rolling around. The thought of the cool tile of the floor against my bare ass excites me now – I think that I probably had an erection at the celebration in the basement.

At about the same age, I was in the dressing room of the local public pool with my uncle, an unmarried, handsome, exciting man. We were naked, drying off after swimming. I stood close to him, my eyes level with his brown, soft cock. It was the first time I ever looked closely at it. I raised my hand to touch it. My uncle said, "That's not right, Tommy." I was embarrassed but not really ashamed.

I remember an unending hard little penis at school, looking at Rubens' women in an art book, seeing a girly picture in the workshop of a muscular young neighbor, and reading about baboon intercourse in an encyclopedia.

When I "got my stuff," I was also hooked on religion in the guiltiest, craziest way. Our family is Catholic and I missed the fine line betweeen passingly proper conduct and actual belief. My religious mother was even opposed to my fervor. Life was confusing. My first orgasms were experienced as teethclenching struggles with the devil, which I lost. My form of masturbation was rubbing, which I still prefer. I didn't learn how to masturbate with my hands until I was twenty-two. My masturbatory images were of wholesome, well-built young Catholic Daddies screwing the hell out of their stacked wives. I was obsessed with confessing to a certain young priest.

Then I forgot about religion and had fun. My favorite game was getting between my mattress and the box springs and rubbing, pressing in. I nastily got cum all over my bedding whenever I got off. My sex thoughts were of guys in Speedo bathing suits. I was a competitive swimmer – I trained in the morning and hung out at the pool all day. A boy there who was my age, thirteen, with a massive physique and a big cock told me about fucking a certain girl who also had a massive physique. I bravely asked him if he would let me fuck her too. He told me I didn't understand about such things. He once bragged that his brother, a beautifully built high school senior, could get it up and shoot off in twenty seconds, that they had contests. I adored the thought of it. My own brother was very distant and busy.

I went to an all-male high school, read French symbolist poetry and began to worry about homosexuality. I talked about feeling queer to one priest who told me that the guys really liked me but thought I was aloof. He didn't say anything about the queerness. The two guys he mentioned as wanting to be better friends with me both turned out to be gay.

And then my family moved from the Midwest to the South, into a mountainous area. A feeling of freedom soon came to me in the new region, at fifteen. I got into hanging out downtown that first summer and I knew I was looking at guys, hoping to have sex. I met an old guy with a huge prick, in the bus terminal, who took me to a gas station john and wanted me to suck, which I didn't want to do, but it was the first time I touched a cock. I tried without success, to fuck a female dog that summer. My brother took me on double dates — I felt my date's tits while he fingerfucked his date. Talking about it afterwards with my brother was the good part.

I also discovered the books of Jean Genet in the library. Reading them made me wonder about my own feelings.

The next spring I was hanging out downtown around sunset and met a man in his early twenties from New York. He was short, pudgy, charming, funny and had thick lips. The two of us kissed forever in a small park, deep and sloppy kisses.

I also became a volunteer tech worker at the University's theater that spring. I lusted for one of the actors. Fate gave me a chance to get close to him, a small chance, but I pushed and got it. I was hired to work at a summer theater with him. He was six years older than me, tall, slim, blond, with a large frame, a manly face and, as I discovered later, a large uncut cock. I stayed as close to him as I could. That is, I bothered him a lot. He was afraid of this demented jailbait, but was also very tempted.

Finally, one night, he invited me to visit the cabin where he stayed. We went up the mountain, sat on the porch and drank beer, saying nothing. He leaned over after a decent but aching interval to put his hand on my leg. He said, "Well?" Kissing, holding and caressing – which to me was tickling – it took hours before I got to the point where I sucked my first cock. I got off by rubbing my cock on his belly after I swallowed his cum.

Whenever he would let me, I gave him blowjobs exactly as he liked them. At the end of the summer, he had me fuck him, as a reward I guess. He was quite grim about it. He told me afterwards that he thought anal sex was a bad practice, but it was the only reason he kept Cornhusker's Lotion around. I loved fucking his ass. I got very enthusiastic and pumped him hard. He made me slow down.

Our affair, romantic from my side only, continued through that winter and the next summer at the theater. I left my family and lived in a garret that winter, getting into various kinds of trouble, including seducing another boyfriend of the big blond actor – the one for whom he did have romantic feelings.

When I was on a visit to New York City with some school buddies, I picked up a stranger who was in his twenties. I sucked his cock, with my buddies, who were probably gay, in the next room. Essentially, I hooked for a place for the group to stay. They pretended not to notice and were glad for the warm floor. Our host was an actor who later came up to the school to visit. I let him fuck me. It hurt. He loved it. That's all I remember. He wrote me a lot of letters, but I didn't answer.

On a summer visit back to the South I stayed in a cabin rented by an older friend, a bisexual man with whom I had bellyrubbing sex infrequently, with no pressure. He felt that it was important that I make it with a woman. That was pressure. He set me up with a very cultured girl whom I already knew. She was plump but small-titted (she wore a padded bra; I was disappointed). Her face was lovely and full of feeling. I took her clothes off, laid on top of her and kissed her. There was a certain inspiring quality to her creamy body but no excitement for me. I played with myself, got hard and fucked her. She rolled her eyes – she'd wanted me for a long time. I mostly liked telling my friend how well I did it.

I had a handsome boyfriend (again, my elder) later that summer with whom I had little sex except for shared visits to a robustly obese, huge-breasted, sloppy-cunted voluptuary with a great sense of humor – an American Rubens. We both fucked her. She, and the situation with my friend, turned me on a lot. We drank rum and felt artistic. I visited her alone twice.

On my trip to California I met a man who fell in love with

me and wrote me long poetic letters. He begged me to let him visit. I did. We had had very moving sex once in California. When he arrived, I felt pleasantly suspended. He flattered me a great deal. I wasn't in love with him but I liked him, our sex and what he had to teach me about literature and politics. We stayed in my dorm room for a while with my sweet, straight, drug-crazed roommate, then got our own apartment. I fell in love very slowly and deeply. He was twenty-four. I was twenty. He was tall with a large frame, ever so slightly pudgy, but strong, and his face became breathtakingly beautiful to me as I fell in love. He fucked me gently with a long, thick fat-headed cock. I fucked him back. We'd both been fucked before but never pleasurably. Our sex was affectionate and non-aggressive. We talked a lot, very sweetly, while we did it.

My initiation was complete.

I lived in New York City now. I enjoy casual sex from time to time, mostly sucking and getting sucked. I like to sell my cock sometimes too. I feel ready for a lover and able to enjoy life without one.

I have sex with a wonderful friend as often as his fear of a binding relationship will allow. I have known him for two years. He has wiry hair on his head and body. He's hard, short, big-armed, chesty and proud. His nice cock gets so full it bulges in the middle.

He enjoys control in sex. He holds me, strokes me, tickles me, works my tits, slaps my ass and kisses me until I am quivering, then shuddering, then purring. He takes my cock in his mouth and sucks expertly almost to orgasm as prelude to his cock in my mouth. I open my throat to take him all the way in. He fucks my mouth, straddling my face while I'm on my back or holding my head as I kneel and he stands. He holds his cock in my throat until he knows I must breathe. He asks me how I like it and I tell him I like it a lot. He tells me how much he likes to hold it in my throat. He stands above me as I lay on my back, his cock over my face. He displays himself, holds his cock down so it points to my mouth, strokes himself. Our sexual relationship went from being intense to being nearly intolerable on the day when he confessed that his secret desire was to have someone beg for his cock. He loves to hold his cock just at my lips and smirk. I love to tell him I want it.

Our sessions last for hours, ending with his amazingly hard cock in my ass, me on my back with my legs up. He enters me gently, using olive oil. When he's got me loose, he teases me by holding his dick barely inside my ass and then slowly filling me with it. Sometimes he will take his cock out and stand stroking it, inquiring about the degree of my desire to have it pounding inside me. He likes my capacity to take him for a long ride. As he fucks, getting closer to his big splash, I feel a release of my entire body that I obtain in no other way – an orgasm that goes on and on and is different from shooting, the fabled female capacity which is perhaps not exclusively so. He is very excited by my pleasure, proud that he has brought me to it and I'm proud that I've pleased him.

On a good night, he'll rest with his cock inside me and start slowly again.

SPANKING EXPERIENCE

I don't know if other readers who are into spanking remember the exact time in their lives when they got into it,
but I do. I can also remember the spankings I got before I
was into it. Boy, was there a difference!

I can remember many times when my mother was giving
me and my little brother a bath together when we splashed
water out of the tub and she stood us up and smacked our
bare wet bottoms until they were red and we were crying.
Those spankings didn't turn me on.

I remember being about five and playing with my little
brother in the backyard. When I hit my little brother with a
clod of dirt, my father came out of the house, stood me up,
yanked down my pants, and lay into me with a eucalyptus
switch until I was howling at the top of my lungs. That switching
didn't turn me on.

And then I can remember when I was six and had an "accident" in bed one night. The next morning, it was my father
who woke me up and saw that I had wet the bed. He dragged
me into the bathroom and got the hairbrush and used it on
me after he pulled my pajama bottoms down and turned me
across his lap. That didn't turn me on.

The spanking I got from my father when I was seven was
the one that did it. It was a Saturday and I had spent the
morning with my friends fishing at the old canal down the
street. We had decided to go to the park that afternoon, but
when I got home and asked permission, my father said that
I couldn't because company was coming and I had to stay and
play with their son.

The company came and I was out in the front lawn playing
with their son when my friends came by to get me. I wanted
to go so bad that I just didn't think. I ran out of the yard and
went to the park with my friends.

Of course I had no fun at all in the park because I started
thinking about what would happen to me when I got home. I
spent the whole afternoon trying to figure out a way to get
out of the spanking. But I couldn't. To make matters even
worse, I was so slow in getting home that it was past dark by
the time I got there. Staying out after dark was a spanking
offense when I was seven. I was in real trouble and I knew it.

When I got in the house, my father grabbed me and dragged
me over to the sofa and stood me beside him as he sat down.

He gave me a long lecture about disobeying him and staying out past dark. My head was down because I knew I was wrong and deserved what was going to happen. He concluded his lecture by telling me to pull down my pants and bend over.

I begged him not to spank me on my bare bottom, but he replied that if I didn't pull down my pants he would and would take off his belt, too. I felt humiliated having to pull down my pants in front of my mother, who was watching, but I didn't want the belt, so I did. When my pants were at my ankles, I suddenly got the bright idea that my underpants didn't have to come down since he'd only said my pants, so I jumped over his lap with them still on.

It didn't work. My father yanked my underpants down as soon as I was bent over. For several minutes, I had to lay there, my buttocks totally exposed to my parents' view, while he repeated my offenses and explained the need for this punishment. Finally, it started.

His big hand sure stung as he whacked me again and again and in a move to defend myself I put my hand back to protect my bottom. I got my hand hit so hard I let out a yelp that stopped him long enough to check my condition. He said I was okay, then started spanking me again. I was wiggling and squirming all over his lap while he spanked. I begged him to stop, promising that I'd be good. But he kept on until he was satisfied I'd learned my lesson.

As he let me off his lap, I kept bent forward so my parents couldn't see my cock because by that time I could feel it was hard. I didn't know why it was hard, but it was and I feared if they saw it I would get more spanking like I had already gotten.

I managed to get my pants and shorts on without them seeing and I went to my room, where I had to spend the rest of the day. In the mirror on the back of the door I could see how red my behind was when I pulled my pants down. I also saw how stiff my cock was. I lay in bed, on my stomach, rubbing my freshly spanked bottom and wriggling my cock into the mattress because it felt so good.

I didn't get all that many spankings after that, but when I did, it was just the same. By the time I was ten, the spankings had stopped altogether, until one day when I was fourteen and my father caught me taking money from his wallet. That time, I got whipped with his belt on my bare ass and when my cock got hard I was old enough to masturbate later in my room, thinking about what he had done to me.

12 Lessons In S&M

B Y   T. R.   W I T O M S K I

I. THE CONSENT

"I want to have you trained. Do you consent?"
"Yes."

II. THE ORDERS

I am alone in a dim hallway. I try the door behind me through which he had brought me, but it is locked. I panic. I shout out his name. There is only silence in reply.

Footsteps come toward me. Two men appear, dressed alike: boots, leather pants, black hoods with openings for their ears, eyes, noses, and lips. They seize me and half-carry, half-drag me along the hallway, down a flight of stairs, and into a room.

One of them speaks to me: "Do nothing until you are told to and then obey instantly. Do not speak unless you are told to."

"But he..."

A whip lashes against my Levi-covered ass.

"Shut up!"

III. THE STRIPPING

"You will stand up and strip off your clothes. If you are not naked in sixty seconds from the time I say go, you will be whipped until you are naked. Go!"

I scramble to get out of my clothes. I get my boots, jeans, jacket and T-shirt off when the voice says, "Time." I am still wearing my socks. The whip crashes against my bare legs, leaving bright red marks. I cry out, but the whip continues to fall. At last, I am naked, and the whip does not fall on me again.

"When you are dismissed, your clothes will be returned to you. You will have no use for them until then."

IV. THE POSITION

They explain to me that when they are not using me, training me (which is really for the sake of humiliating me, and not actually training), or allowing me to sleep, I am to spread my legs and bend over. My hands are to part my ass cheeks so that my hole is exposed. I am then to kneel and lean forward until my forehead and shoulders rest on the floor. It is a position I had better get used to, they say, since I will be spending many hours in it.

V. THE BOOT SERVICE

Already, they are becoming interchangeable. There are at least five of them, possibly more. I can no longer tell one from another. I understand: I am to consider them all merely reflections of the man who brought me here. I am to serve them as I would serve him.

While in the position, out of the corner of my eye I see a black boot. Almost instinctively I move so that my lips can touch it. Becoming bolder, I let my tongue dart against the leather. If I am not to do this, then I will be punished. When no whip, belt, hand, nightstick, or riding crop strikes against me, I allow my tongue to run more freely over the boot.

I let go of my ass and grab onto the boot, licking the dust from it, working on it, slurping, sucking until it glistens with my saliva. I turn my attention to the other boot. I don't dare focus my eyes on anything but the pair of boots I am servicing. After a long time, the person in the boots appears to be satisfied and he leaves. But another takes his place. My tongue and lips grow numb, but I do not allow my tempo to flag. I'm intoxicated by the smell of leather. It's a very potent aphrodisiac; my cock is hard. The hours drift by.

VI. THE THROATING

His nuts are the size of billiard balls. His cock is enormous, rockhard, long and thick. He guides my slobbering mouth along the shaft which shoots a good nine inches from the forest of black pubic hair, burying my face in that hair, forcing my nose to deeply sniff his odor, pushing me beneath his balls to smell the funky sweat, making me lick and suck and take those huge balls into my mouth, before bringing my lips back to the head of his cock. He inserts himself into me. Slowly, he forces his cock deeper and deeper into my mouth, and then my throat, until the gag reflex begins. He stops, but then forces it even deeper into my throat. At last, the whole thing is buried in me, my lips and nose hidden in the cock hair at the base.

"Yeah, that's good."

I feel proud to have taken his cock all the way.

He begins to fuck my face, bucking his hips. Then he stops abruptly, pushing me back to the position.

"Not yet. Cum comes later."

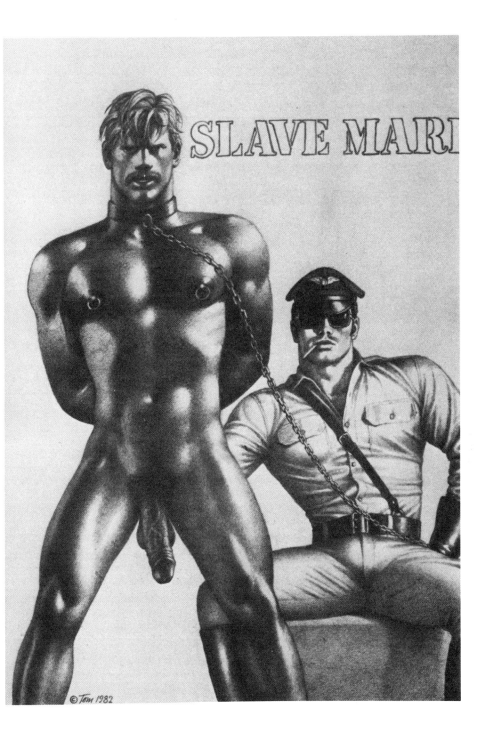
SLAVE MARI

© Tom 1982

VII. THE SHAVING

I see the clippers, soap, and straight razor. I know what they are going to do. I rebel, and yell, "No, please. No." I try to get away, but two of them chain me to the floor. My ass feels the whip. After a few lashes, one of them tells me that the whipping will continue until I beg for it to stop.

I suspect that the man who brought me here has told them that I fear being shaved. It is a strange quirk of mine. Of all possible scenes, this is the one I have difficulty accepting. It is as if by taking my hair they are taking a part of me I do not wish them to have.

Furthermore, the man who brought me here has no doubt told them that for the whipping to be effective, I must beg for it to stop. I am strong, both mentally and physically. I can endure a great deal of pain. I take pain as if it's all a contest: I can take as much as you can give. They give me many strokes before I scream through my tears for them to stop.

The clippers are run over my bloodied ass cheeks. Then, a razor is used on what the clippers missed, going all the way into the crack and around the hole. My legs are clipped, too. Then I am turned over and the rest of my leg hair is gone. My chest hair. The hair of my armpits. My pubic hair. My cock looks even larger now. My body is felt, not — I know — for my pleasure, but so they can admire the barber's work. My cock is throbbing hard.

Then they cut the hair on my head so short that what remains is just stubble. But they leave one segment long so they can grip it.

VIII. THE CHAINING

They put me down on my back. They fasten leather bands around my ankles. To the D-rings in these another chain is fastened, joining my ankles, while still another chain runs to a collar they have placed around my neck. The chain from my ankles to my collar is so short that I will not be able to stand.

They tell me that when I am finally allowed to rest, I will not be able to stretch out my legs. I whimper. They laugh.

IX. THE FUCKING

I feel hands on my ass. A finger, soon followed by another, and then another, slides inside my hole. The fingers find and caress my prostate. Pleasure streams through my body. I moan and thrust back to get more, when suddenly the fingers withdraw. I sigh in frustration.

"Loosen up, faggot. I'm gonna put my cock up your ass. When we're finished with you, you ain't gonna be satisfied unless you got a man's big cock down your throat or up your fuckin' ass."

He shoves his enormous hardness into my tight hole. I cry out in pain. He holds still. When the pain turns to pleasure, he slides the rest of his cock into me. I feel stuffed with cock, overwhelmed with cock. His fingers play with my nipples. I wiggle my body, impaled on that giant shaft. He makes a dozen full strokes, pulling almost all the way out of me before battering in again. Then he draws out. I moan with relief and disappointment.

The opening is re-stuffed with a leather dildo. The dildo is narrowed at the eight inch mark so that the sphincter muscles will grasp it, making it impossible for me to eject. I am fucked with the dildo. I am told that it is my duty to desire it.

X. THE CLEANING

Leaving my ass plugged, he squats before me, his legs spread, his impressive cock standing hard and ready.

"Get your mouth busy."

I turn my head away. He slaps my face hard, forcing my unwilling mouth open, and shoves brutally down, past the blockage where my mouth joins my throat, burying all of his cock's inches deep into me. I buck and twist at the invasion.

"You took it before; you'll take it again. Clean that cock!"

Tears in my eyes, my face red from the lack of air, my tongue works to clean his cock.

XI. THE TOILET TRAINING

They have me chained in a bathtub. I am their toilet. They piss on my naked body. When so instructed, I open my mouth and drink the urine that floods me. My body is soaked and surrounded by piss. My cock rises above the yellowish water.

XII. THE RELEASE

"You've got a choice to make. To be free or to come with me. What is your decision?"

"To go with you."

An Enema From His Father

B ecause of your feature on virgins in the second issue of *FirstHand*, I decided to write about how I lost my virginity to my father when I was a teenager.

My mother deserted my father and me, leaving my father to act as both parents. Although he worked as an ironworker, he tried to meet all my needs, both physical and emotional, while ignoring his own. He never went on dates or saw women, coming home to look after me after work.

When, one day, I stayed home from school complaining of a stomach ache, he decided that the best treatment for my condition would be to give me an enema. First, he explained what he was going to do, and then he led me to the bathroom, telling me to undress and position myself on the bathmat, in a knee-to-chest position with my ass high in the air. Saying that he didn't want to mess up his trousers, he removed all his clothes but his shorts. As he filled the hot water bottle with a soapy water solution, he explained how he had often given my mother enemas in the past. Hanging the filled water bottle from the towel rack, he got a jar of Vaseline, gathered a glob of the slick stuff on his fingers and started to rub the opening of my anus, telling me to relax. As I started to relax myself, I could feel his fingertip push slightly inside of me. Gathering more of the stuff, he pushed his fingers further inside me. Although his finger felt strange, I became excited, causing my penis to rise.

When the finger was withdrawn from my behind I actually pushed back, trying to recapture it, only to have it replaced by the douche nozzle instead of the regular, smaller enema nozzle. As the value was opened, letting the warm water flow, I almost came, shoving my ass back, wanting more of the nozzle inside me. Noticing my excitement, Pop started to move the nozzle around inside of me, asking if I was enjoying my enema. All I could do was groan and mumble, thrusting myself back and meeting his forward thrust with that piece of plastic. When I had taken all the water, he told me to go to the toilet and empty myself.

As I hurried to the toilet before I made a mess, I noticed that he had an erection, with a wet spot at the point where his penis was very obviously protruding in the shorts.

Like all teenage boys I knew a little about homosexuality. Sitting on the toilet, I thought of my reactions to the enema, as well as my father's own excitement. I wondered if he wanted to fuck me or if the memory of giving enemas to my mother was what excited him so much. While I was sitting there he came into the bathroom, telling me that he wasn't going to work but had an errand to run. He would be home in about an hour and told me that once I was through in the bathroom, I should go back to bed and rest.

When I returned to my room, I brought the Vaseline and the nozzle. Coating the plastic nozzle with Vaseline, I shoved it up my ass, fucking myself with it, dreaming of me and my dad together.

My father came in silently and saw what I was doing. Without a word, he got naked and showed me his big erection. I was excited being caught like that. He got onto the bed and withdrew the nozzle from my ass. I was on my stomach with my legs spread in invitation.

Rubbing my back and buttocks, he asked if I enjoyed the feeling in my ass. When I said that I did, he asked if I'd like to have him instead of the nozzle fucking me. Once again my answer was yes. Then he asked if I ever let any of my friends play with me or fuck me. This time the answer was no. He shoved a finger up my ass and asked if I was sure I wanted him to fuck me. Pushing back hard, I yelled, "Yes." At this point he reached over, got the Vaseline, and rubbed huge amounts of it on his cock.

He rolled me onto my back, placed his arms under my knees, and raised them almost to my chest. He told me to place his cock against my asshole and to tell him if it started to hurt. Once in position, he slowly pushed himself inside of me, stretching my ass to its limit, but with no real pain, only a warm feeling of being filled to capacity, stopping every once in a while to let me adjust to his size. Just as he had completely buried himself in me, he let out a deep sigh. He paused briefly, only to slowly retreat until just the head was within me. As his speed increased, so did my excitement.

I started to tell him to fuck me harder and faster, until my cum erupted, splashing off his hairy stomach and chest. Then I felt his climax erupting inside of me. I could feel the spasms deep inside of me. After we had both come, he collapsed on top of me, still buried deep in my asshole.

From that day until I started to go to trade school, we usually slept together. Now, some seven years and many lovers later, my father is still the best. I thank him for showing me a way of life that I had wanted to discover.

FETISH EXPERIENCES

Ripped Denim

Why don't you ever run any articles or pictures of guys in ripped jeans or T-shirt? There is nothing more exciting than seeing a hunky guy walking around with a torn T-shirt – especially across the pecs so that his nipples pop out – or with a big rip in the ass of his Levis, so you can see one hairy bun. I also like jeans that are real worn in the knees, because then I can fantasize that the guy who's wearing them has been down on his knees sucking cock so often that he's worn them through.

Whenever I go out barring; I always wear a torn T-shirt and Levis with the ass hanging out, and a frayed spot right over my basket, so if you look close enough you can see the head of my cock peeking through. A lot of guys are turned on to the scene, and the best sex I ever had was with a dude who was dark and tall and lanky, sort of like a young Tony Perkins – a real turn-on for me. This guy was wearing jeans that were all worn away at the cuffs, and the side seams were splitting every few inches, so that you could get a quick glance of his hairy calves and thighs whenever he moved. The pants were split right up the crack of the ass, and I started to get hard just thinking about how easy it would be to fuck him without even pulling down his jeans.

He was wearing the rattiest Levi jacket I've ever seen, worn out at the elbows, and the collar half torn off. One of the pockets was missing, and that was hot too. Underneath was a T-shirt that was practically in shreds, and I was turned on by the overall image more than I've ever been before. I guess he was too, because he came over and started a conversation.

Later, after we talked a while, he joked that we must go to the same tailor, and when we got home, we didn't take off anything but our jackets before we got it on. Things eventually got a little rough and I started to rip the T-shirt the rest of the way off him. The more I ripped, the more turned on he got.

Pretty soon he pulled out his prick and started beating off. I took one of the strips of the torn T-shirt and I tied the fabric around his prick and balls like a cockring. That just about drove him crazy. He was tearing at the basket of my pants, and he didn't even try to unbutton the fly. He just tore at the frayed spot until it ripped open, and then he pulled out my cock. I let him suck on it for a while, but I had other plans for him. Before he knew it, I was fucking him right up through the rip in the ass of his jeans.

It was a dynamite scene. and I don't regret it for a minute, even though the front of my Levis were so badly torn that I could never wear them out in public again. Sometimes, though, around the house, I'll put them on, with my cock hanging out. If I'm in the mood for a hot jack-off in front of a mirror, those ripped up pants will do it for me every time.

Military Training

I lived in Baltimore for the year I attended college there. I was 22 and had a really hard body. My lover at that time was a 34, and wore his hair real short, in military fashion. He took me to a barber in downtown Baltimore's sleaziest section, and for a dollar, I, too, was given a crewcut that passed the old Army regulations code.

My lover loved the military scene, in detail. The basement of his house was his "playroom" — converted into a barracks. The first time he brought me down there, I was really stunned. There were narrow cots in a row. There was a flag down there, and the rack with uniforms and other military paraphernalia.

His mood turned serious, even strict. He told me that I was to get dressed in a complete privates' uniform, including lace-up boots, Army belt, and cap. There was a complete uniform there my size. He told me that I was not to overlook any detail of authenticity. Dog tags were essential and they were hanging on a nail over my cot. There were even Army issue boxer shorts for me to put on.

He shoved a pair of tall, black Sergeant's Boots in my gut and told me to have them spit-shined by the time he returned. He told me I could find some good jerk-off material under the flat matteress of my cot, to pass the time until his return. He turned without saying another word. As I heard him climbing the stairs and closing the door to the basement behind him, I wanted to call back to him, but I didn't dare. I had my orders to fulfill. This was the Army.

A mirror was hanging on the wall of the dimly lit barracks, and it was splattered with dry cum. I watched myself in that mirror as I discarded my civilian clothes and became a soldier. With each article of the uniform that I put on, I fell more into the mood.

There was a boot shining kit on the floor, and I used it to polish his boots, spitting on the black leather to give it the extra shine he demanded. My cock was hard as I rubbed the rag back and forth over the boot toes. It made me think about the porn books he'd told me about under the mattress.

My heart was really thumping because at least half an hour had already passed, and he still hadn't returned. But I looked through the pages of the magazines that were under the mattress. They were cheap beaver shot magazines of whorey women and some of hustler-type boys. My dick was oozing into the boxer shorts and into the uniform pants.

The door upstairs opened, throwing a shaft of light down into the barracks. His footsteps were heavy and deliberate. He was wearing another pair of boots. I was about to say something when he yelled, "You stupid dog. You new recruits have got a lot of learnin' to do, don't you scumbag?"

"Yes, sir." I knew what to say, instinctively. But my response was not loud enough. He cuffed me on the side of the head and told me to repeat it. Then he saw the magazines on the cot. "Jackin' off when you were supposed to be shining my boots, boy?"

One action led to the next, until he had me tied down on the cot with my fatigues and boxer shorts pulled down to expose my naked ass. He stayed in uniform, with his dick out of the fly of his pants, while he fucked me, all the time telling me in my ear that he hoped for my sake that the other guys wouldn't come back to the barracks to find me getting it up the ass.

I think that both of us actually became the fantasy characters of our minds in that uniform scene, and in the other uniform scenes that followed. Over the course of our time together, we played out a variety of roles in Navy, Air Force, and Marine uniforms. We eventually went our separate ways after I moved out of Baltimore, but I felt that I had also been through military training, as far as his uniforms were concerned. Even though it was only a small part of my life some years ago, I do miss the uniforms and the Drill Instructor who took me through my paces.

"It Looked Like a Rose Bud"

*T*he best sex I ever had was when I was twenty and living with my widowed mother in her apartment. She was still teaching then and went away to a teacher's meeting for a few days.

For some time I had been watching the married policeman who lived across the hall from us. He was a real handsome guy, built like a million dollars, and really filled his pants out in such a way that you could tell he had enough to feed the poor for years and years. When he would bend over you could see what a nice pair of buns he had. No mistake about it, Steve was a real hunk. I had talked to him a few times and we always seemed to hit it off. I was working that summer so had time to spend doing nothing on the weekends.

His dear little wife had gone away to visit her folks in another state and left Steve on his own. He had weekends off so he was going into his place when I happened to be coming in and we stopped to chat. He kept looking me up and down and asked me all kinds of questions – if I was doing anything special, etc. I told him I wasn't, so he asked me if I wanted to come over and watch some TV with him; there was a football game on that afternoon. I jumped at the chance.

After a few beers, he offered me a sandwich. It was a hot day and we each had only a shirt and pants on. He stripped off his shirt and said it was okay for me to do the same if I wanted. I had a feeling this was leading up to something, so I went with the tide, loving every moment of it. After eating what he had fixed, he offered me a fancy drink, and then told me the drink made a person horny and sexy – then he winked at me. The party started to get hot after that drink. He was talking sex, telling me all kinds of dirty stories, and prancing around showing off his build.

Finally, I had to take a piss, so asked him if it was okay. "Hell, man, I got to go also. I'll show you the way," he said. I walked into the bathroom and he was so close behind, it was like I had a shadow. I pulled out mine and started to urinate, and he had his in his hand, standing right beside me, and let fly into the bowl. "Kinda fun to do it together," he said, putting his arm around my waist. I loved feeling him that close. I didn't even have time to talk, for he had finished and turned me around to face him, and he planted a big kiss square on my mouth. I loved the way he put his tongue in my mouth

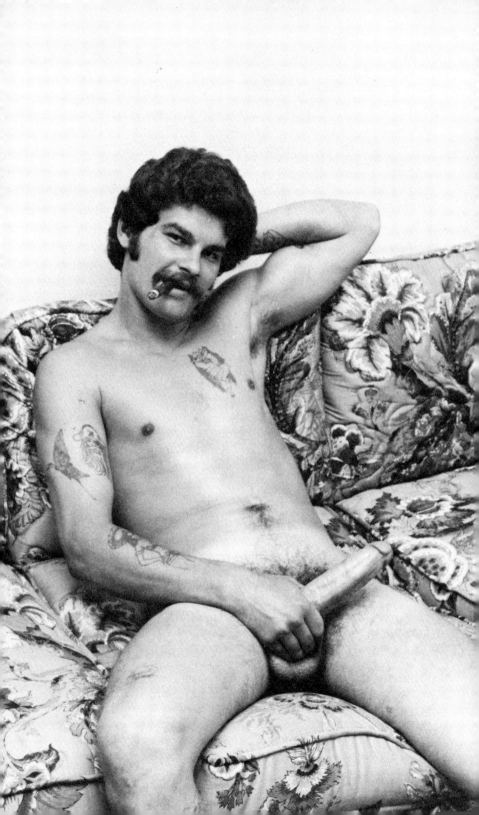

and was rubbing up against me with his cock half-hard.

After that long, loving embrace, and our tongues fighting a duel that sent my blood pressure up he whispered to me: "Let's take our clothes off and get it on. Okay?" I kept wanting to slow down and take it nice and easy, even though I was no virgin to all of it. He told me that he hadn't had sex for a week and had been jacking himself off twice a day.

The rod he had on him was white and uncircumcised, with the skin nestling up around the pink head of it so that it looked like a rose bud. It was a good eight inches just soft, and I could see he was a full-grown, healthy stud ready for action. He told me he never cheated on his wife but with me he was not doing anything wrong, for he had a right to enjoy sex with another male if he was handy and safe.

He asked me if I ever had sex with another man. I told him that I was into it a little but did not consider myself ready for the trash pile. "Not with that body and what you got going for you between those legs, kiddo," he replied.

We lay on his bed side by side with hard-ons and he rolled over on top of me and told me he wanted to just hug me for a while. This was okay with me. It seems he had picked up on my mood of wanting to go easy and enjoy it. We talked and told each other lots of screwy things and how we liked to be touched and so on until we both felt really turned on.

I loved it then when he started to tell me what to do — to command me. He told me to lick his underarms, and do a good job on his tits, and not to miss the navel with my lips and mouth. "I want you to give your ole' man a tongue bath, sonny boy. Take your time and do not miss anything. If you do I'll have to punish you good and that means a spanking, you hear?"

He pushed me down to the foot of the bed and told me to lick his feet and when I had done a good job of them I could continue on up his legs. By the time I got to his hips he would be ready to come and I would be giving him a good blowjob, taking it all the way down my throat and when he blew his load I could swallow all of it. I was happy as a kid in an ice cream parlor and did just like he told me to. I did not rim him out, but did kiss around his ass. When he spread it, he told me that I was going to be fucking it that night, so to be thinking about that.

I think I would have just let it burn rather than give up one single moment of that bliss. His voice, his touch, and the smell and feel of him was like magic to me and I was on clouds floating in space. Looking into those eyes and sensing what he was thinking told me he was as high on this whole experience as I was. No drugs — just pure sex between two healthy young men who were turned on to each other. Everything I did to him, he did to me that day. As I look back on it now a good deal of it was mental, for we talked a lot and told each other how we felt.

I gave him a blowjob that was so good I never wanted it to end. He really was good at giving his cock to me; gentle, yet firm and commanding. Sticking it all the way deep into my throat but taking it out so I could get my breath and telling me he did not want to hurt me and if in any way it was too much to let him know. He kept me going this way for at least an hour before he shot his load. All the sweet cum I swallowed was like nectar of the gods. He held his dick in my throat so I could really drain his nuts dry. Then he pulled out and kissed me on the mouth, hugging me close to him.

God, he was good; the best. After months of watching him come and go, walking around in his uniform with that gun and nightstick on his belt, I thought, "This must be a dream, and I never want to wake up." When he was shooting his load, he was saying, "You cocksucker, you love it. You know that you do and I'm going to give it to you good." That was a real turn-on for me.

After a shower and a nice rest, we slowly went at it again and this time he wanted to fuck me. I had taken only two other guys in my young life then, but my ass must have been made for such, for I was able to take him right up to the balls and it felt good to me.

He was a good fuck and had greased me up good, so it went real fine. I had taken a good wash-out so was real neat for fucking. Slow and easy, and then faster and firmer, riding me real good so I was begging for that dick up my rear end. "Give it to me, Daddy," I told him. "Nobody can do it like you do it. I love you."

That was the best night of my life, and as I look back on it now, it was really the best sexual experience I ever had. Steve was a good lover and a good man. He could not get over that time we had and wanted me time and again. We had to be very careful after that, for his wife returned the next day. He told me he thought about me all the time. I asked Steve to give me a pair of his used underwear and a sock, which I kept as a reminder of him and of that first time with him.

ORGASM EXPERIENCE

Tim: A Problem Orgasm

I read with great interest and anticipation of your forthcoming article on male orgasm. I hope you will include in it an examination of the orgasm experienced by a very small percentage of males (5% or less) as described by Kinsey in his famous work. For these men, the achievement of orgasm is usually labored and prolonged. Once reached however, the orgasm is violent, often overpowering, characterized by an almost totally rigid body, gasping or irregular breathing and, as ejaculation begins, some or all of the body muscles spasm or convulse rhythmically, coinciding with each spurt of semen.

I am one of these men and, while sex remains a beautiful experience, there have been certain problems. I'm writing to you to shed some light on them and perhaps to help someone out there who is like me in this respect.

My thirteen-year-old cousin and I brought each other out a few months after my fourteenth birthday. The happy event occurred on the large iron bed in our attic one warm afternoon that Spring. We had gone up there to change into our swimming trunks. However, as we stripped, latent feelings and desires began to assert themselves. In a few minutes, we had yielded to them completely and were lying side by side. Sex evolved and it was beautiful, natural and innocent.

Physically, my cousin and I were quite similar; the same height and weight, our hair slightly different shades of light brown, and both circumcised. Whether because of our shared bloodline or merely by coincidence, we also experienced orgasm in much the same way. From that time forward, we would spend weekends together, always feigning sleepiness in early evening to get to bed sooner.

With the bedside radio softly playing music, the warm yellow dial light would cast a pale glow over our naked bodies. Having not as yet been intimate with other boys or young men, neither of us saw anything unusual in our intensely rigid bodies, taut quivering bellies and spasming muscles. When it was over each time, no questions needed to be asked. Each would survey the disarray of blankets, the scattered sperm and his panting partner and say, "Whew! You had a good one!"

My cousin, though younger, was more adventurous. After a session of strip poker with one of the neighborhood boys, he made a classic seduction. The next time we were together, I received a report on his conquest. The boy in question was big, circumcised, quite uninhibited sexually, but came copiously and did so calmly, relaxed, with a faint smile on his face. He also could not understand why my poor cousin took so long to come, and when he finally did, why he indulged in such "theatrics."

Some time later, when I was a high school senior, I at last began to branch out sexually. My first "score" was unplanned, totally spontaneous and very similar to my cousin's in its outcome.

It came about because a member of the school's swimming team and I were assigned to work together on a science project. This called for us to work together an hour or so each week, outside of class. So it was one noontime we dropped by his house for lunch and found nobody home.

"I'm not very hungry," he said. "Why don't we just goof off for a while?"

Upstairs in his room, we looked through his old junior high school annuals. He pointed himself out in a photograph, in the front row of the swimming team. "Wow," I said. "You had muscles even then."

Then, after a long pause, he asked me which of the boys in the picture had the best build. I pointed to a blond on the right whose broad shoulders and concave abdomen were obvious, even in the photo.

"Yeah," he said, quietly. "And I remember he had quite a muscle...down there." His finger lingered, marking the center of the blond's swimming trunks.

"Yeah, you can tell," I ventured in a shaky voice. "But I bet this guy has him beat." My finger came to rest on the boyish image of my science project partner. There was a long, almost unendurable pause as each waited for the other to speak. My pulse pounded so loud I was sure he could hear it.

Finally, he leaned near me and, in a low whisper close to my ear said, "Do you wanna get naked and give your milk?"

He helped me undress, his hands running freely over me. I laid back on his bunk and watched as the physique I had seen soapy and wet so many times in the school showers was revealed again to me. The shorts were cast aside and my eyes were drawn to what they had concealed. The pink head was already protruding from the sheath of skin that had always

40

hidden all but the tip from view.

I remember still the complete charm of his warm, smooth skin upon mine, pressing me down on the bed. He cradled my head in his arms and lowered his face to mine. My eighteen-year-old heart knocked wildly against my ribs. It was the first time I had been kissed while naked. Locked in his grasp, I was swimming in ecstasy as his muscular bulk moved with ever-increasing urgency upon me.

Suddenly his surging movements stopped, and he whimpered as wet warmth flooded between us. After a few minutes, he lifted his weight from me and rolled on his back exhausted, his hand covering his eyes. At length, he sat up on one elbow and, with evident displeasure, saw my unserviced cock, alert and throbbing.

For him the excitement was over. He was grimly determined to get me off and out of there. He dipped his fingers in the pool of cum on my belly and applied it roughly as a lubricant. He grasped me firmly and began to pump. The veins in his arm stood out as his rhythm increased. I cried out from the near-pain and begged him to stop, but he continued, his face dreamy and indifferent to my agony. Finally, almost in tears, I "gave the milk" and he released me.

After a moment, he bounded from the bunk, found his shorts and slipped them up and on with a loud snap. That was that. Hurt and still dripping, I dressed, all the while hating the person who was standing in his shorts, combing his hair in the mirror.

Graduation followed soon after this humiliation. I made preparations for college, thrilled at the prospect of new beginnings with exciting new friends. After a while, the memory of the swimmer faded. When I last heard, he had become a used car salesman.

Because of a college ruling, all freshmen had to stay in the dormitory or other supervised housing. So, for a frustrating year, I remained abstinent. The tantalizing aura of maleness, everywhere around me, drove me to almost perpetual masturbation.

I frequented the library, reading everything I could on the subject of homosexuality. There were a number of older books on the subject and, though out of date, I absorbed them all, searching for clues about the gay lifestyle. In particular I was looking for some safe, sure-fire way of telling who was gay and who wasn't. The books weren't much help on that or any other point.

I found the Kinsey Report a bit later and at last understood something about my orgasm, and why my cousin and I had trouble with other boys. My big problem was, and remained for some time, the ignorance of my sex partners.

In my sophomore year, I decided to put an end to my frustration or die in the attempt. I left the dormitory behind me forever and took a one-room apartment just off campus. It was seedy, rundown and overpriced. But I was preparing for great sexual adventures. It was paradise to me!

However, since sex requires two participants, searching for that certain male, out there someplace, began to dominate my thoughts and fantasies. I was still too much the innocent to realize it was all around me.

One rainy Friday afternoon, I decided to wash some clothes and clean house. The apartment building provided a community wash facility complete with the familiar pay machines. With a basket of laundry under my arm, and quarters in my jeans, I went down there. Just outside the door, in the darkness of the basement hallway, I collided with another resident. laundry scattered everywhere; he tripped and fell into it. Both of us were laughing hysterically as I helped him to his feet. He was a smallish guy with blue-green eyes and hair we used to call "strawberry blond." I was transfixed by his golden aura.

We gathered all the laundry into one sodden pile and carried it into the washroom. There we played a game of "Sort the Shorts." When I found some of his, I wished mightily I could discern something of his sexuality by some tiny clue, detected with casual unseen glance. But they looked just like mine.

His name was David, a recent transfer to the business school. He was from a large urban area in the Southwest. His personality and disposition matched the sunny climate that had been his home. He was at once my best audience, drawing me out, laughing at my jokes, bringing out the best in me.

When the washing was done and everything neatly folded, we left. Our happy chatter was unabated down the corridor and up the stairs. My fascination with him was complete. I was powerless to break away as we came to my door and went on past, up more stairs to his door.

He asked me if I had any early classes the next day. I shook my head and shyly continued to linger. "Tell you what," he said, tapping his chin with his doorkey. "It's such a long way back to your apartment, and it's so late. Why don't you spend the night with me, and you can get a fresh start in the morning?"

My thoughts raced. I swallowed once and finally managed a semicalm, "Sure." Becoming reckless, I added, "It might be fun." He swung open the door, and I followed him in. The door closed with finality behind me and suddenly I felt a wave of panic, of unpreparedness.

He dropped his laundry basket down on the floor and walked to the windows. "You have everything you'll need with you," he said, drawing the first blind all the way down. "No need to worry about that."

I was still the innocent, searching for confirmation without saying too much myself. The best I could manage was: "Do you have an extra set of pajamas?"

"Pajamas?" he echoed, exploding in laughter. "I don't wear pajamas and you won't want to either!" He drew the last blind down and made no move to turn on a light. Cool darkness filled the room. I made out his silhouette against the dim glow from the windows.

"You see," he said, stepping nearer, his voice husky, "Guys like us don't wear pajamas when they sleep together. When I have a special overnight guest like you, even shorts get too warm."

My broadening grin of comprehension was matched by his own smile. He answered the question I couldn't find the words to ask: "Sure I am, brother. And so are you. You want it bad, don't you?"

"God, yes," I blurted.

"So do I. It's been weeks. Come, get me."

I started to cross the room, but my foot caught in his laundry basket, and I flopped helplessly into the sea of underwear, towels and socks. David stood over me, laughing until there were tears. Seizing his arm, I pulled him down onto me.

With shouts of laughter, shrieking and screaming, we rough-housed in the snowy playground on the floor, each trying to undress the other. Buttons popped, shirts, shoes, socks and finally pants flew through the air in wild abandon. Now, just shorts remained. Our giggles diminished. At some point, wrestling slowed down and became caressing. The golden vision, open and submissive before me, filled me with awe. The generous chest, the flat belly, all overlaid with copper colored down, glowed like a sunset. My hand strayed to the elastic of his underpants to make the final unveiling.

Gently, he stopped me. "No, wait. Shorts are sexy."

So, for several minutes, one last flimsy barrier between us, we necked, petted and kissed with increasing excitement, until the fabric, stretched almost to the point of tearing, became slick and semi-transparent.

At last, the need to come raging inside, a quick flurry of arms and legs rendered us naked. Wild with passion, we embraced and shuddered with the delicious shock of skin on skin. Our hands and mouths explored freely; we nuzzled each other's chests, then abdomens. At last, mouths on target, my tongue explored his pink plum and I tasted the sweet, salty slickness that oozed from him. My own body warned of impending orgasm, as his lean hips stiffened and I received his warm essence in my mouth.

Then I was seized by my own contractions and the spasms that followed. Bucking and bouncing against David's still ejaculating body, he gasping and sputtering, I returned the sperm he had given me. Finally, the convulsions lessened and the contortions subsided. We lay still.

David's face was frozen in a shocked smile. In the violence of my first spasm, I had literally bucked him out of position. His mouth had lost its grip on me, and my rampaging cock had soaked him with semen.

"Ooo-wee. Ride'em, cowboy," he said, softly. "The next time we do this, I'm going to have to remember to hang on!"

"I'm sorry," I began. "It's really something I can't help."

David found a towel. He dabbed at his face, neck and hair. "Don't be sorry. I loved it, really. I must be hot stuff to make you do that. At last, I have a talent for something!"

He tossed the towel aside and, lying back, closed his eyes for a few moments of rest. He had seemed so much the skinny boy with his clothes on. Now, with nothing to hide his splendor, my eyes roamed over the small, muscular man's body beside me. A thin trail of fiery red hair led from the tight navel downward to the thatch of darker hair. There, delightfully disproportionate, nature had given him the equipment meant for a football team's fullback.

David's appearance was deceiving. While he projected the image of the naive, innocent boy, he was a street-wise, self-accepting, totally knowledgeable homosexual man. He loved life and the sexuality that was an inseparable part of it. With David, it was okay to laugh in bed.

Over the next three years, we learned from each other, our sexual styles evolving. The saddest day of all came much too soon. With the diplomas in hand that each could not have gotten without the help of the other, we saw each other in the crowd and edged closer to speak. We promised to write often, perhaps visit back and forth, and then we turned and ran. Men aren't supposed to cry in public.

A job took me to a distant Northwestern city. I soon found and entered gay society, forming a circle of warm, caring friends. I began to attend parties and would rejoice each time at how many men there were of my persuasion. It was hell when I had thought I was the only one.

At one such party, given at a recently restored Victorian mansion, I encountered the usual faces and the usual cigarette smoke. Judy Garland blared forth from the sound system. Wine glass in hand, needing fresh air, I explored other rooms.

I came across a charming panelled library. My hosts were fond of first editions. I browsed the titles. There was even a section of ancient volumes devoted to the study of the homophile. Many of these were familiar to me from my days as a sex-starved college freshman. The eighty-five-year-old multi-volume *Studies in the Psychology of Sex* was there. My fingers ran down the row, searching for my favorite volume, and found it missing.

From behind me, a voice spoke up: "If you're looking for *Sexual Inversion,* I'm...I mean, *it's* over here!" A man about my age was seated in a wing chair by the fire, the book open on his lap. He looked over his glasses and smiled.

We introduced ourselves and I sat in the chair opposite him. It was then I recognized him as a member of my class in college. We had never met, had seen each other only in passing, running to this class or that.

We talked about the book a bit and I fondly recalled it as something of a "shocker." The case histories proved what was obvious, I suppose: That men wearing handlebar moustaches and nothing else made love by gaslight in that so-called "innocent" time so long ago. They did what we do now, and did it with equal enthusiasm. The people on that bicycle built for two just might be two loving men!

I had found some of the Victorian prose amusing and some of the case histories highly erotic. The book was considered "reference" material by the library and could not be checked out. I confessed I would take the book to the basement of the library, find the most secluded part of the "stacks" and seek out those passages for prolonged study.

His eyes widened with disbelief. "You did? I used to do that too! I wondered why the pages were stuck together!" We laughed at our little shared secret. One by one, our inhibitions fell away.

We began to share something of our backgrounds with each other. As we did, curious coincidences came to light. We were born in the same town at the same hospital. We were born just ten days apart. The same doctor had delivered us and tended our aches and pains up through high school. Yet, because our homes were fifteen blocks apart, we went to different schools, had different friends and pursued our sexual awakenings without the other's help.

Curiously, our lives had so loosely intertwined, each just missed the other time and time again, until that night. The talk was good and later, over wine brought in by one of the servants, we began to probe our deeper thoughts, our hopes, our goals, our fears.

I was moved by this strong, yet very vulnerable man. The sense of growing intimacy was undeniable, not just sexual, but mind to mind, a fusing of spirits – friendship. I wanted to say something, but my mind was drained of words. Finally, I just blurted out, "I wish we'd bumped into each other down in that damned library basement!"

He smiled brightly and nodded vigorously. Our eyes met. Wordlessly, *the question* was asked and answered. Later, in the car on the way to his house, we scarcely spoke. Our hands met. This was going so well, I didn't want anything to spoil it. I closed my eyes, took a breath, and decided to risk one more confession. "There's something I think you should know about me," I began.

"Oh oh," he said, and slumped in his seat, looking out the window.

"It's just that I love your company very much and I don't want you to be surprised or turned off by something." Feeling very self-conscious about using such terms out loud, I explained what happens to me during orgasm.

"Oh, *that,* " he interrupted, relief evident in his voice. "I already knew that!" It seems he had slept with one of my old boyfriends who had mentioned it and "thought it was quite a coincidence."

The dashboard lights revealed his growing smile. "Coincidence?" I echoed.

"Yeah. You're not the only one. I jerk around a bit, quite a bit when I'm in bed with someone I especially like."

Over a whiskey at his house, we talked further. As we drank, the conversation slowly turned to sex. We compared notes on how the orgasm felt and what it caused us to do in a frenzy. Warming to the subject, we spoke at length about the "beached-fish" syndrome and the shock it created for some of our bed partners.

Rolling the whiskey glass in his hands, he expounded a theory: "Guys like us have a tendency to become too rigid as the climax approaches. We fight the orgasm. We fear it. So, it takes longer to happen. We think we completely lose control of our bodies, but we don't, not entirely. I've found you can greatly maximize the pleasure by forcing yourself to relax a bit just before it happens. That way, muscles are not so tensed, the messages get through, and the orgasm flows over you, gripping you completely. It can be very, very wild."

Finally, nervous anticipation began to show. Our hands shook and the rattling ice cubes betrayed them.

He rose to his feet, took my glass and said, "C'mon. Let's play doctor." I rose and followed him. As we crossed the room, he hooked his hands under his turtleneck sweater and, with a single graceful movement, slipped it off and dropped it to the floor. My throat tightened at the sight of his broad shoulders and slender flanks. I gulped and threw my suit jacket and tie in the same general direction and followed him up the stairs and through a door.

It was not his bedroom, but a sort of guest room, sparsely furnished. At one end was a low double bed. He made the room ready, drawing the drapes, turning on lights and starting a small electric heater.

We said little as we undressed, savoring the age-old ritual cherished by gay males the world over. Soon the golden moment was at hand. The last flimsy garment slipped to the floor and we drank in the vision of each other's nakedness. We embraced, kissed deeply, and rubbed together in the world's oldest dance.

New pressure made us back away a bit. We looked down and smiled, glad to see we were, after all, still growing boys. Curious fingers explored, retracing the faint lines where, twenty-six years before, our doctor's special scissors (probably the same pair) had marched around, rendering us safe and hygienic for the vagina we never had the interest to seek out and penetrate.

Now fully erect, we positioned our hips so that we touched tip to tip. We smiled at each other across the not-quite-half-yard that separated us.

After a moment, he turned and removed the covering from the bed. It turned out to be a bare mattress on a low sort of platform. The mattress was old, stained and spotted with the

47

remnants of past ecstasies. With a firm hand on my shoulder, his other outstretched, I accepted his invitation and reclined upon it. Smiling, he crouched beside me and began a slow, sensual massage.

I felt myself relaxing and coming under his control, his soothing words of praise and assurance almost hypnotic. My eyes closed as I felt the cool lubricant being applied. Slowly, very slowly, he began to squeeze and stroke. There was no sound but the soft slurping of the lubricant and my increasingly labored breathing.

In a few minutes, I was writhing under his masterful, feather-light technique.

He grasped me with both hands and encouraged me to thrust while he held still. I watched the swollen, shiny cock head appear and disappear between his thumb and forefinger as I thrusted, giving myself even more pleasure and torment.

He knew my body and its responses as if it were his own. He played me like an instrument and I responded with ever-increasing enthusiasm. All the while, he coached me, took charge, bringing me time and again to the perilous brink of climax. My pubic hair became matted and black, soaked with lubricant and pre-cum. With his free hand, he explored behind my balls. A finger entered me, found my prostate and began a gentle massage. I gasped for air and struggled with the new sensations streaming through my body. Words were impossible; I tried to moan but a curious strangled wail was all that came out. He spoke in a low, calm whisper: "When you feel it, relax, accept it, welcome it." He increased his rhythm slightly. My breathing all but stopped, a loud explosive gasp every fifteen or twenty seconds was the best I could manage. After a minute, he spoke again, softly but very firmly, "Okay. Big breath. *Big* breath. Let it out...Relax!"

My internal organs began their contractions. Waves of sensation swept over me. My back arched into the climax. My head snapped back, my mouth and throat forming a silent scream, as bright flashes of silver-white sap arched through the air. My body jerked and bounced helplessly on the mattress, my arms and legs dancing in time to the spasms of my erupting penis. I seemed to be floating free, out of my body, observing myself.

Soon though, the tumult had passed and I sank back, panting and gasping. With soothing words, he eased me through the body shudders and cock twitches, the "aftershocks" we experience. Then, this too was past. With a gentle squeeze, he milked my softening penis of its last drops then with several tissues, began to clean me. The mattress and the wall behind it would dry by themselves. At last he laid the soggy tissues aside and positioned himself between my legs. There was a moment of exquisite pain. My smile flickered but remained. I welcomed him, longing for the physical union that would symbolize our growing bond.

Moist and blinking, our eyes met and held. He reached out his hand and brushed my messy hair. I held his fingers and kissed them. Wordlessly, another question was asked and answered. Our mouths opened to each other and his warm body enveloped me.

That was fifteen years ago. "His house" became "our home." Our hair is getting grey on the sides and we have to watch our weight more carefully than before. Sometimes bed is just for cuddling and sleeping but, all in all, I wouldn't have it any other way.

"Doctor, when you said you wanted my husband in bed for a few days, I thought..."

High School Fantasies

W hen I was in high school I used to have fantasies about our football coach. His office, where I spent a lot of time while I was a student, was off the locker room and there was a small bathroom with a toilet and a ceramic tiled shower just off his office.

In my fantasy, I obediently walk into the coach's office at exactly eight o'clock. He was always very strict about punctuality. The shower area is dark; only the office is lit. I sit at the desk. He takes his clothes off and sits on the desk with his feet on the arms of the chair. He then pulls my head into his sweaty crotch. His hog of a cock rubs over my face. I suck his cock, lick around his balls and clean his asshole with my tongue. His thighs are strong and my tongue easily glides over his powerful muscles. His cock is full, long like the rest of his body, meaty. My mouth is full, but I can't seem to get enough of it in my mouth. I want more.

The head of his hog is thick, like a fist. He pulls my head away by my hair and gives me some poppers which send me into a frenzy. All I want is that cock, to suck and lick his balls, to clean them with my mouth. As the poppers wear off and he begins to withdraw, he starts to piss just a little bit to give me a taste of what's to come.

Three men walk into the office carrying a case of beer and a brown bag. My coach and the three guys begin a hearty drinking party and I am removed from the scene at this point.

My coach, Cal, takes me into the side bathroom and tells me to take off my clothes. He's going to make sure I'm clean for his friends. I lay on my stomach, naked on the ceramic floor, as he quickly rubs Vaseline around my asshole and gives me an enema. He checks to make sure I am clean by sticking a tampon up my ass and then removing it. When he is sure that I am clean, he tells me that I am just there to be used by his friends. We then go back out to his office.

The lights are dimmer. The men are high from the beer; they are naked and sit around the office, laughing. It's a party and I am there for the same reason the beer is.

One of the men grabs me by the ass, slipping one finger into my hole as he pulls me toward him. Again my face is in another crotch. Another hog of a cock is filling my mouth. One of the other men shakes up a beer and pushes the long neck of the bottle up my ass. My balls begin to throb. In Seattle we have a beer with a neck on the bottle that is about six inches long.

By now I need to use the toilet. The air is full of poppers; the scent of men is all around. The bathroom is just barely lit. As I sit there, one of the men comes in. He faces me and says that he also needs to piss. His cock is thick and long and he aims for my face, pissing right into my mouth and then onto my chest, over my stomach, and onto my cock which is now long and hard. As he splashes the last drops on me, he stuffs his hog into my mouth and tells me to lick him clean, which I do. He then pulls me up and holds me under the shower.

The other men have now come into the dimly lit bathroom. Cal gives me a beer. After having a few more, I am told to get down on my knees and suck one of the men off. More poppers. As I get into sucking this man's cock, I can feel Vaseline being put on my ass, then a couple of fingers being shoved into my ass. Out of the corner of my eye, I can see a huge dildo being pulled out of the brown bag. As it is shoved into my ass, I feel as though I am going to break apart. It's pushed in and out. More poppers. The man's cock I am sucking is now beginning to pulsate; spasms of cum fill my mouth and easily slide down my throat.

The dildo is removed from my ass; two fingers, three, four, the fifth and then a fist is formed in my ass. More poppers. They are all tightly holding onto me as the fist is being shoved into me. Cal says he needs to use me to piss. The fist is removed and his big dick is stuffed in. His piss is hot. My dick begins to spasm. I feel as though I am flying. Another cock is pushed into my mouth. I can feel piss spilling out of my ass. Someone says, "The only way to relieve a stiff dick of piss is to stick it in a hot ass." Cal continues to pump his hog in my ass, his hands gripping my tight thighs. I can feel his dick getting harder with every stroke, faster, harder. His body seems to be getting taut.

Another man sits on the floor. Another man is stroking his hog next to my face. My ass is pumped full. My face and mouth are covered. I lick every drop up. Cal removes his cock. I lie on my stomach, facing the man whose dick I have been holding and I suck it into my mouth. More poppers. Back on my hands and knees. A fist is again shoved up my ass, with a cock in my mouth. Once again, Cal beats me off.

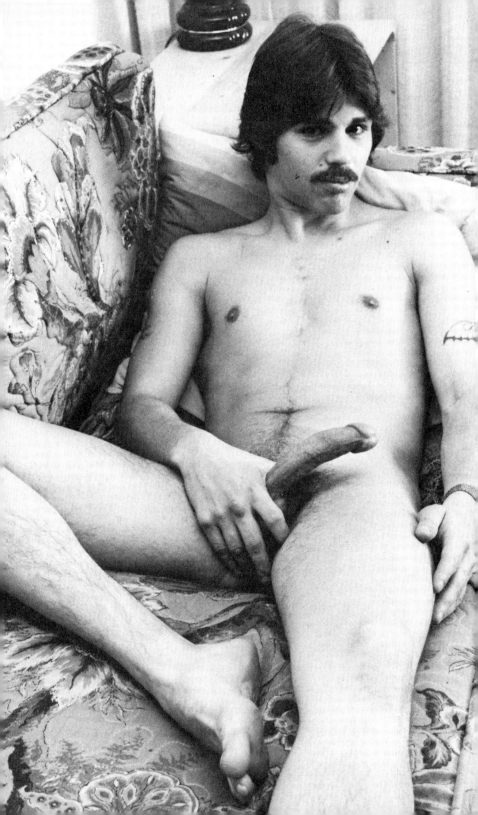

JACKING OFF ALONE

Clark

*M*y favorite technique for bringing myself off is anal masturbation. The methods used to stimulate my asshole and prostate have been developed and refined over the years. It started when I was thirteen, during an every day jerk-off session with a friend. We were jerking and sucking each other off to orgasm even before we could shoot. One day, my friend eased a finger up my asshole while he was sucking my cock. He hit the magic button and I exploded with a fierce cum. We both developed asshole techniques on each other to enhance our sex play. Surprisingly we did not fuck, but used fingers, vegetables, and whatever else we could think of, in our asshole, to supplement our sucking and jerking off.

Now I have an eight inch latex cock, which is six inches in circumference. It is about an inch longer and about the same thickness as my own erect cock. I get myself in the mood by playing with my cock for a half hour or so. Then I fill a used Fleet enema pack with warm water and shoot it up my asshole. This is normally repeated three times. I shit this out and get ready for my action.

The latex cock has already been prepared by fitting the full length with a condom. A good amount of K-Y is applied to my asshole by one, two, and then three fingers. Incidentally, the rubber is used on the dildo to reduce the effect of the corona ridge as it goes back and forth past my sphincter. Without the rubber on the dildo, I tend to bleed; with it, I can fuck myself for an hour or so.

I find that the best place to do this is in the shower stall or bathtub. In the stall, I crouch down with a mirror aimed at my asshole, so that I can see the cock going in and out. The pleasure derived is exquisite because I have full control of the action. The prostate contact is in my hands — fast or slow, hard or easy. When I get really turned on, my sphincter muscles try to reject the cock. This is the most pleasurable part in forcing the cock past the resistance. Unfortunately, I am unable to maintain a hard-on during this plunging. I lose complete bladder control and piss randomly. It is not easy for me to come this way, but about half the time the sensations are so great that I shoot off with a soft cock.

I have been fucked with a live cock perhaps fifty times. While this is enjoyable, there is no comparison to my own latex fuck. By necessity, I limit fucking myself to once per week. The asshole needs time to get back to normal.

—Illinois

Bill

Masturbation has been a big part of my life ever since I discovered it by accident when I was thirteen. Of course, since I had had no sex education from my folks, school, or church, I thought this must be really damaging. But it felt so good, I did it anyway — frequently.

I've become skilled at beating off. I have a nice 7½" uncut cock, and since it gets down to a very small size when it is not hard, it is a pleasure to just watch it grow and achieve its full perfection. I would say that my cock is really good looking, and could easily be a star for porno magazines. I enjoy it, and everyone who has ever seen it, sucked it, or played with it, marvels at it. That makes me feel good.

As I said, I'm uncut. The foreskin is great to massage over the head when it's in my pants. When I'm reading *FirstHand* in my office, I love to work my meat in this way. I can bring it just about to the explosion point, but then hold off and keep it inside for a while. Then the chills of sexual excitement that sort of creep all over my body, especially over my shoulders, can be enjoyed many times before shooting.

If I'm in my office, I'll probably have to go to the men's room to bring myself to completion. The best way is to just pull back the skin, hold on, wait, looking at the throbbing perfection and the beauty of it. Then I delight at the explosion of cum. Oh, man, what a feeling!

Sometimes I like to work the foreskin back and forth rapidly. That brings a good jack-off, but I think it's better just pulling the skin tight and letting the juices spill.

One of the favorite positions I know for a good jerk-off is on my stomach in bed, with both hands on my cock, again pulling back the skin and exploding all over the sheets. This is especially fun when I'm in someone else's bed (i.e., a hotel or motel), and want to leave a little reminder of my sexy presence.

I'm married and can function with my wife (although I don't

consider myself bisexual at all). I have really loved the times I'm with a man, and we have great gay sex. But, really, I guess I can just about bring my cock to its fullest experience and feeling. I guess I know it best.

One thing more: I love to rub my finger on the edge of the glans, especially at the bottom where the split is. It causes a wonderful, burning sensation, and the feeling goes down to my feet. If I rub the left side of my cock, it burns down to my right foot; if I rub the right side of my cock, it burns beautifully down to my left foot. I've often wondered if everyone is like this, and if uncut cocks have more feeling on the edge of the head than cut ones do.

I love the smell of an uncut cock. I keep clean, but at the end of a sweaty day, it's wonderful to smell that manly, strong odor from my hardening meat as I begin stroking it in another wonderful jack-off experience.

I love your great magazine. By the way, I'm a pastor.

—*Iowa*

Steve

*I*n your Fall '82 issue, there was a letter from someone who wanted to know how to do auto-fellatio. I've been doing it since I was sixteen, and I am twenty-seven now. I discovered how, quite by accident. I was jacking off, while lying on my bed, and the thought occurred to me to find out whether I could suck my own cock. The thought got me quite turned on, and shocked me at the same time.

I swung my legs over my head. It seemed rather logical. But, I couldn't reach the head of my cock with my tongue. I probably would've given up, except that I was on my bed, and my bed was in a corner. I put my head on my pillow, and I was close but not quite close enough. Then I got the idea of using the corner. By pushing my feet on the walls, with my legs over my head, and gradually lowering my feet, I did it! First, I just got my head in my mouth, and then about two inches. I was getting so turned on, just by the thought of what I was doing, that it didn't take long for me to shoot my load!

I'm not exactly super limber, and not super long. The keys to doing it, for me, were a pillow and a corner. If I can do it, I don't see why anyone can't. Often, on other occasions, I'd just shoot all over my face.

—*Michigan*

Rich

*M*y favorite masturbation technique is to position a mirror by the side of the bed to show my asshole, and then to insert a dildo up my ass. I oil down my long dong, and slowly fuck myself with the dildo as I stroke my cock in rhythm with the fucking strokes.

When I get hot and ready to cum, I sniff a little amyl and shoot a load of white cream all over the mirror, a couple of shots landing on my face so that I can taste my own juice.

I've been masturbating since I was twelve, and this is the greatest turn-on of any of the techniques I've tried. I've also enjoyed sucking my own cock over the years, and drinking my own juices when I do. I love the taste and the sweetness of another man's juice, but there's nothing like tasting my own.

–Florida

Chris

I wonder how many of your readers have tried a masturbation technique that I discovered a few years ago. While swimming in a hotel pool, I discovered that it was very arousing to direct the jet of warm water that fills the pool toward my groin.

One night I was having a late swim and was the only person in the pool. It was possible, therefore, for me to drop my trunks and let the jet of warm water play directly onto my erect cock. I can't tell you what a marvelous sensation that created. The continuous movement of water playing against my rock-hard shaft was a feeling I had never experienced in any other sexual act.

With a slight movement of my hips, I could whip my cock back and forth from side to side, in the water. The most arousing thing was when the jet of water directly hit the underside of my cock head. I kept this up for a long time, getting close to orgasm, then backing off and cooling down a bit.

Finally, I couldn't hold back any longer and gave in to the pleasure of one of the most fabulous orgasms I've ever had. It was fun, also, to watch the jets of cum hitting the jet of water and being immediately scattered out onto the pool. You can be sure that, after that, I found many opportunities to swim in pools where I was the sole occupant.

I'm sorry I have to remain anonymous.

—*Texas*

Kenny

I purchased your magazine for the first time today, and have already read it cover to cover. It is an original.

I'm writing this in answer to the letter asking about auto-fellatio. I am adept at this unusual form of masturbation, and have been doing it for about thirty-five years (I am now fifty-three). I started it as a consequence of an incestuous encounter with my mother.

Although my penis is just six inches, I can easily reach my penis and envelop about half of it in my mouth. There are two positions I use for auto-fellatio. One of them is the "plough" position of Yoga – this is the heels-over-head position. I do this, but I prefer the sitting position. I often prepare for auto-fellatio by taking a hot bath to relax my back muscles. Then I stimulate my penis until it is standing up stiff. I sit on a bed or sofa with my legs crossed, and I caress my cock and balls some more to keep it up.

Next I begin slowly pulling down. I don't touch my cock sometimes until I have pulled down several times. I "pull down" by wrapping my arms around my middle thighs and pulling. A beginner should go slowly. After a few "pull downs" I touch my glans with my tongue or my lips. It is only a matter of time until I have the whole glans in my mouth. At this point, it begins to feel good. Then I start to swing on myself.

When I get to really sucking myself, I can do prodigious things. I lock my whole cock and balls. My glans is soaked with my saliva. I lick the sensitive underside of my shaft. I fuck my own cheek. I can do wild things. Auto-fellatio is great when I've smoked so pot.

At first I did not swallow my own semen. I had had some homosexual scenes as a kid, with other boys. We did a lot of things together, but we didn't swallow semen. But, eventually, when I tried it, I found swallowing to be the best part of auto-fellatio. When I am going down to the maximum on myself, I feel myself throb, and I know just where to lick to trigger myself to a mind-blowing cum.

Most of my orgasms really are mind-blowing. I try to orally contain my bucking, orgasmic cock. My eyes see – out of focus – the throbbing pulse of my orgasm. Sometimes I bite my cock in the frenzy of orgasm. Sometimes I keep on sucking. When I'm really feeling high and really into it, I'll just keep on sucking until I empty my balls completely.

I have had very few homosexual encounters in my life. I suppose this is one of the disadvantages of auto-fellatio; it has made me an introvert. But my auto-fellatio is always a source of novelty. I always know that – with little effort – I can have dynamite solo sex. I never get tired of it.

I have done it in hotels, motels, pullman cars, standing in the toilet of a 747 airplane. I've done it sitting on the ground in the forest. I did it as a soldier in the war. I was never discovered, though once two drunken friends burst into my room and caught me in my underwear, supposedly sleeping, but with the tell-tale odor of fresh cum on my breath.

Anyone who is slim with a long torso should be able to perform auto-fellatio. There is a form of self-hypnosis involved. It is a very intense and a very satisfying form of solo sex. I would love to form an auto-fellator's society, if I had the nerve to do it. We are, after all, a minority within a minority.

"You blew the mating call and got me all horny for NOTHING?! Bend over, lover boy!!"

"His Cock Was Uncut & Smooth"

I grew up during the Second World War when most of us kids had fathers or older brothers fighting in the war. The war was part of our lives and games, even though it was thousands of miles away. We even read comic books about the war. Among our favorites were the stories about the underground resistance fighters who would sabotage the Nazi war bases, and later get caught by the Gestapo and tortured. All of us kids planned to join the Army or the Secret Service as soon as we were old enough.

Our most popular war game, a variation of a traditional boys' game, was called *Gestapo*. The two oldest and toughest kids around, usually Mike and Jack, who were my secret heroes, would each pick up teams of about four. Sometimes others could watch. One team, the Saboteurs, would have a secret and the other team the Gestapo, would try to find out what it was. The secret would be in three or four parts, something like "The Main Street Bridge is to be blown up at midnight." Except for the leader, each Saboteur would only know one part.

After a slow count to twenty, the Gestapo would try to catch the Saboteurs, not always an easy job, and then torture them into telling the secret. The game would end when the Gestapo had pieced together the secret or when a half an hour was up, in which case the Saboteurs would win. The Gestapo would usually hunt in twos or threes, and when they caught a Saboteur they would drag him back to "headquarters" and tie him to a tree for questioning.

The tortures were usually pretty mild. We never allowed ourselves to do anything that would really be harmful or leave noticeable marks. Besides you have to stop when the Saboteur gave his secret or began to cry. No punching or kicking was allowed and almost everything that worked was soon taboo or restricted. It got to the point where the Saboteurs usually won as the Gestapo could not get the whole secret.

It was at one of these games that I got to know Arthur. He was a wiry, blond boy, fourteen the same as me, but built smaller. In fact, he looked over a year younger. For some reason I felt attracted to Arthur, while at the same time I used to put him down. He had a pale, almost translucent skin which seemed to glow when he was angry or excited, and which let you see the veins and muscles in his arms.

Arthur would sometimes hang around me at school. I would tell him to scram because I didn't want to be seen with little kids. I did once give him a nickel to play pinball.

At the time, I didn't know much about sex except that the older boys fucked girls, and sometimes did it to us younger kids. I had only been "done" once and that was by my uncle who lived on the rich side of town and went to college. It hurt quite a bit, and it was only because boys were supposed to be brave that I didn't cry. He gave me a good licking afterwards to make sure I didn't tell on him.

One day, while playing our game, I was a Saboteur, and Arthur had helped Mike, the Gestapo leader, capture me. Arthur was given the honor of torturing me because I had accidentally kneed him in the gut during capture. He was hurt and angry, and Mike told him to really let me have it.

Mike always spent more time watching or torturing Saboteurs than in trying to catch them. He was a big, stocky, really tough sixteen-year-old, who was always in trouble with the police. He would let us younger kids punch him in the stomach three times as hard as we could. I once saw him take a long hat pin and shove it through his bulging bicep. He also liked to squeeze kids in the balls, but that wasn't allowed in the game.

The Gestapo had already found out the other two parts of our secret and knew that I knew the last part. Jack, our leader, hadn't been caught and there were only twelve minutes left. Arthur started with the usual arm twisting, Indian sunburn and tit pinching, even though you were only allowed one minute to do it. I had kept my sweater on just in case. The Gestapo was not allowed to reach in or take off any clothing. Then Mike urged Arthur to belt me.

Under our rules, the Gestapo was allowed seven smacks on the bum with a belt. Only once had this ever made me talk, and that was when the Gestapo was allowed ten. I figured I could hold out easily. So far I had pretended that Arthur's efforts had caused me more amusement than pain. Mike tied my arms over the trunk of a fallen tree and held my feet. Then Arthur took off this heavy army belt that his big brother had given him. I got excited and I think hard as he prepared to take his first swing. Only the tip caught me, but Arthur's pants fell down to his knees and everyone, especially me, laughed.

Mike urged him on, making him take twenty second pauses

between strokes. The remaining six smacks were really hard as Arthur worked out his frustration. The pain overcame the excitement, but I felt good because I had taken it bravely without even flinching. I mocked Arthur and was thinking of the fun I'd have the next time when I got him.

Then Mike decided that, seeing as how I had kneed Arthur, he should get to give me another seven smacks. I was almost sobbing by the tenth blow, and everyone could tell. While I didn't tell my part of the secret – didn't dare after laughing so hard – I felt very ashamed. Crybabies weren't even allowed to watch our games.

An hour later, after some pop and pinball at a corner store, we started another game of Gestapo with the teams reversed. I was really eager to prove myself. I captured the smallest Saboteur, a cute dark-haired kid named Jamie, and watched while he was tortured. He didn't last very long, but he took quite a bit of punishment.

Jack held Jamie down while another boy did lip stretching, shoulder chops and arm twisting. They had started on some heavy tit and belly pinching by the time he gave up his secret. He had held out for almost four minutes. If it had been any less than two minutes he wouldn't be allowed to play Gestapo again. I even helped capture Mike, the Saboteur leader, but I didn't bother, or maybe dare, to torture him.

Then all by myself, I caught Arthur, who was hiding in the farthest corner of the block. I even managed to get his arms tied behind his back with the rope that we Gestapo carried. I became almost uncontrollably excited, and instead of taking him back to headquarters as we were supposed to, I decided to torture him right there. I was able to tie him to the rear support of a billboard. I started with tit pinching, but he had on two shirts and wriggled like hell.

Then I remembered his belt, the heavy army one which he had used on me. I tied him up higher and pulled off his belt. His pants fell down to his thighs exposing his pale, lean buttocks. In the backlight of the sun, I could see peach fuzz on his bum. I suppose I should have pulled his pants back up, but I was overcome with the idea of smacking his bare bum with the belt. I ordered Arthur to tell me his secret, hoping he would refuse so I could at least smack him a few times. I still, however, wanted to get his secret so our team could win.

He refused and even swore at me. I slowly meted out seven of my hardest smacks while he struggled. His bum became red, really red, but all he did was turn his head and spit at me. Then I retied him facing frontwards, undid his shirt buttons and started tit pinching him again. This time he couldn't wriggle as much, and with no clothes in the way I could really dig in with my thumbnails. I was hurting him, but he remained defiant although there were tears in his eyes.

Arthur's dangling, half naked body glowed with rage in the sun. I was tempted to squeeze his small, hairless balls, but I was afraid to touch him there. I had already broken several of our taboos, and I didn't want anyone to think I was queer. He had noticed the bulge in my jeans anyway.

In my deepest, sternest voice I told him I would make him talk. I twisted his sorest nipple. "You can't make me," he screamed, and he spat in my face. I decided to give him another seven smacks because he spat at me. I took my time to get the most out of it. Arthur just gritted his teeth and took it without struggling. His bum turned even redder and I could see large welts forming. At the end, I noticed some blood. That was another taboo; no drawing blood. I had lost. After what I had done, I didn't dare drag him back to headquarters. I untied him and let him go. He spat at me again. I couldn't even feign anger. I admired him for his guts, and tried to say I was sorry.

Arthur called me a pansy and a suckhole, and said I could give it but I couldn't take it. Afterwards he said it again in front of all the other kids. I protested and boasted that I could take more than he could. "Okay, queer," he replied, "we'll take turns smacking each other. Only this time you gotta pull down your pants like when you did it to me. I'll even let you have first dibs."

I had no way out. Mike made each of us in turn pull down our pants and bend over the fallen trunk while the other laid one on. Mike said it would be more fun if we took off all our clothes, but this freaked out almost everybody. It was decided that everybody would get to give the loser an extra smack, except for Mike and Jack, who could have two each if they wanted.

Everyone gathered around to watch. They were really excited. Maybe it was the bare bums. I could see that Mike and another boy had hard-ons. Little, darkhaired Jamie was vigorously playing with himself under his jacket. This was a real test of guts, not just another game of Gestapo.

I began to realize what it might be like to be really tortured. I kept smacking Arthur's raw, bruised bum as hard as I could. I had to make him give in first to preserve my reputation. But he'd just take it without any sign of pain and grab the belt for his turn. I figured he'd probably pass out before he'd give in. My admiration for him turned to awe. I really didn't want to hurt him anymore but I had to try.

Each smack he gave me seemed worse than the one before. The pain spread over half my body, and I felt hot and cold rushes. After Arthur had given me five smacks, I realized I couldn't take much more. I wished I hadn't started the whole thing.

After seven strokes, I was really starting to bleed. Jack stepped in and called a halt. Both of us had had enough. Jack made us shake hands with each other and say, "No hard feelings." I really meant it, and I think Arthur did too. He gripped my hand firmly and gave me a smile. I had wanted to hurt him and I had, but now I was overcome by very different and confused feelings.

Arthur and I became friends after that. He even bought me a milkshake at the soda fountain the next day. His bum was sore for almost a week, not that his parents noticed or cared. He was a tougher kid than me. It was amazing. A younger looking kid was actually my hero and I wanted to do anything for him, to be gentle and kind and sort of loving to him.

I had my own private basement room, and I got him to come over two days after the Gestapo game. I had bought some pop and had stolen some cigarettes and half a bottle of rye from my mom. After a while we showed each other our bruised bums. He said his still hurt a bit; it was covered with purplish blotches and lines. I went and got some lotion of my mom's and he let me rub it on. He said it felt good. Arthur said mine needed some, too.

Soon we were rubbing it on each other's bums. We both got excited. Arthur suggested that we take our clothes off so we wouldn't get lotion all over them. At first I was reluctant because I knew what would happen. I had never been naked in a situation like this before. I had never even touched someone else's cock before.

Arthur said it was okay. His brother, who had given him the army belt, had often jacked off in front of him. And just before his brother went overseas, they had jacked each other. "You hafta practice to be good with girls," his brother had said.

Arthur started taking off all his clothes, and we soon stood facing each other stark naked. I stared at him. His slim body was more muscular than I had thought, and graceful, too. He had a flat, rippled stomach and you could see his muscles under his skin when he moved. His skin was practically white in the dim light. His cock was uncut and smooth like the rest of his body; there were a few dark blond hairs just beginning to show around it.

"Go ahead, touch it," he said. I watched my trembling hand reach out and slowly grasp his hard cock. His smiling eyes told me he enjoyed it. I was thrilled as his cock grew harder in my hand. In wonder I pulled back the foreskin and watched the shiny, rosy head emerge and the veins enlarge. He began to play gently with me and we both eased ourselves onto the bed.

I was almost too excited to stay hard. He stroked my thighs and belly and lightly tugged on my balls and rubbed lotion everywhere. I then poured half a bottle on him and we rubbed it all over each other. We ended up slippery wrestling on the floor, laughing, tickling and teasing each other. We played that way for a long time before we got down to serious jacking. When he finally made me come, I tingled from my belly button to my knees. It was a gusher. When his turn came he squirmed and squealed. We even hugged each other after.

The first couple of times after that, we would give each other a few smacks on the bum with the army belt before bringing out the lotion, but afterwards we didn't bother. At first, Arthur couldn't come even though he got very excited. After about six months, he had almost as much hair as me and could squirt all over the place. We would pretend that our cum was lotion, and we would rub it all over each other's bodies. We'd let it dry, shower together and start all over again.

We even had names for our cocks, mine was Peter and his was Ralph, and we'd make up stories about them. In this way, we would play for hours, each coming two or three times. We also had the usual contests. Once we took turns tying each other, to see what would happen if the other didn't stop jacking after one of us had come. It was too much.

We only played Gestapo a few more times, and avoided capturing or torturing each other. We liked to watch the torturing, especially when the Saboteur was really brave.

One time, Arthur and I captured little Jamie. Instead of struggling and trying to get away, he told us that he could take it on the bare bum just like us. He pulled down his own pants and bent over an old stump. By the second smack — they weren't very hard — he was so excited and horny that we jacked him off instead.

He asked if he could jack us off so he could see what cum

looked like. We took him over to my place and pretended Jamie was our slave. He even sucked our cocks, something we'd never thought of. We then tried it on him first and then each other. Wow! That was neat.

Jamie had really soft, olive skin, completely hairless, and a small, stubby cock with a round knob on the end. You could even get both his tiny balls in your mouth as well. He liked lots of suction, and would finger his asshole while you blew him. He'd get almost violent when he couldn't take anymore, but half an hour later he would demand to be sucked again. He became a nuisance and we couldn't get rid of him for days. I think he also wanted us to fuck him, but we certainly weren't going to get into that.

By the time the war ended, about two years later, we'd had lots of practice. Then my family moved to another city. I sometimes think back to our Gestapo games. Torture only fascinated me when both sides were willing and it was a kind of contest. Real torture where people are helpless makes me sick. I wonder if boys still play these kinds of games today.

—*Vancouver, British Columbia*

"*I don't care if the script calls for me to play a flasher. You're not tying a string to it.*"

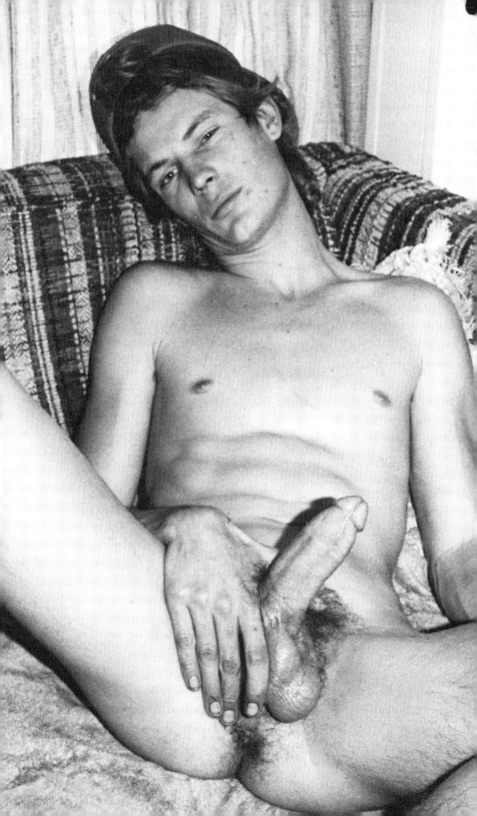

BOYS WILL BE BOYS

Herb

I first experienced pleasurable sensations in my crotch one summer day when I was six years old. I was sitting on the john enjoying the feel of warm sunshine coming through an open window, and trying to have a bowel movement that seemed extra large and firm. As I pushed to get rid of it, the pressure against my young puckered asshole made the whole area down there tingle deliciously. When I released the tension to suck up the bowel movement back inside for another try, it felt even better.

After quite a few minutes of this pushing and pulling to keep the wonderful feeling going, I noticed that my little, hooded prick was standing straight up. Just then my nursemaid knocked on the door and said, "Hurry up. You've been in there long enough. There are other children who need to use the bathroom." For the rest of the summer, it seemed as if the highlight of each day centered around my going to the bathroom. That fall, my next sexually-aware incident occurred. Denise, my babysitter, was taking care of my younger brother, sister and myself. One night while looking at a comic book before bedtime, I suddenly felt an irresistible itching on my uncircumcised penis, and realized it was coming from around the inside of my protruding, rosy, tender glans. I dropped my pajama bottoms, and started to tweak, squeeze, and roll my soft, little foreskin around between my thumb and finger. Oh, my God, what a feeling it was. This action seemed to concentrate a million, electric-like prickly tingles in my stiff, little cock.

I was so mesmerized by this wonderful, new feeling that I never heard Denise come up behind me. Her "What seems to be the matter, dear? had me so surprised, I told her exactly where it itched. She told me to come with her, and that she would try to take care of my problem. After pulling up a chair to the washbowl, Denise told me to take off my pajama bottoms, and step on the chair. I still had a hard-on.

"I think you need to have your little pee-pee washed, so that the itching will stop," she offered. She then ran a warm stream of water to soap up a wet facecloth. Suddenly, an exquisite thrill of unknown anticipation gripped my cock and balls. I stared down at my hairless bone-hard prick, with its miniature, red, rose-budded foreskin gathered at the end, just as Denise encircled me with her arms from the back. The facecloth was in her left hand and her right hand was poised to slide my tiny foreskin back.

She then gently pressed her thumb and forefinger on my still covered cockhead, and started to slowly peel the tight foreskin back. When the glistening, purplish head with its pink, baby slit started to appear, I seemed to suffocate with ecstasy. A warm mass of tiny pinpricks of pleasure made me feel as if my whole being was inside my bursting cock. When my foreskin got to my cockridge, it felt like it could not go further. Denise forced back a little harder, and the slickness of my cockhead let it pop over the cockridge, then settle in a smooth, puffy, snug, red collar around my cockhead's neck.

While Denise had pushed my foreskin all the way back to apply the warm, soapy, facecloth, an intense rush of pleasure nearly made me collapse. This signalled that my first dry orgasm was over. Nevertheless, she continued to sponge my little bone-on.

The dry orgasm, however, had left my cock so sensitive that uncontrollable, short bursts of piss shot out of it as it jerked wildly out of Denise's grasp. She said, "Oh, my dear, I'm sorry if I irritated your pee-pee, but I think the itching should stop now."

That was my first of hundreds of dry orgasms. It took a few years until I was finally able to shoot. God, if that babysitter only knew how incredibly good that had felt, and how exciting it had been for me.

My stiff cock had become soft again as quickly as it had become hard. My clean little cockhead then slipped back inside its tight hood. From that moment on, I knew that I would always be wanting that wonderfully exciting feeling to happen as often as possible.

The only other times that my cock pissed bursts was when someone else jerked me off, and kept jerking my cock for a few seconds after I finished my dry coming. As soon as I started to shoot those first few drops of cream at the age of twelve, I no longer had piss bursts.

—*Bangor, Maine*

Shannon

*M*y first sexual experience was with another boy who was a year younger than myself. I was thirteen and had discovered jacking off about six months earlier, quite by accident. I had played around with a couple of friends prior to this, feeling each other's dicks and such, but nothing more.

I had gone to some people's house one evening with my parents. I had never met these people before, but my parents said that they had two sons about my age, and they wanted me to go. When we got there, the parents settled in for a card game, and I was told that John, their younger son, was out back in the swimming pool. I should go out and introduce myself.

I went out toward the pool, which was secluded with shrubs, and found a good looking boy, with blond hair, skinny-dipping. When he saw me, he got a little embarrassed and swam to the side of the pool to hide as much as he could. The lights were on in the pool and I could see everything. He knew it.

I introduced myself and sat down by the pool. We talked for a while, and I told him not to be embarrassed because I swim naked in my pool, too, whenever I could. He relaxed a little then and asked if I wanted to skinny-dip with him.

He watched as I stripped naked and jumped in. We swam and splashed around for a while. I watched him do some dives that he learned on his swim team. He told me that there was a sauna in the bathhouse and it was neat to use.

We jumped out of the pool and went into the sauna. We lay down to enjoy it. This was the first time that we really had a chance to check each other out. He was slender and very athletic. His dick and balls were pretty well developed for a twelve-year-old. He had even started sprouting pubic hair. Being a year older, I had a little more hair down there, and was a little bigger also. While we were looking and not saying much, we both started to get hard.

John asked me if I jacked off. When I said yes, he reached over and started stroking my dick. It felt so much better to have someone else doing it for me that I was in complete ecstasy. I just lay back and let him do whatever he wanted. Pretty soon I got that familiar feeling. I shot jism all over my belly and his hand. It was the best feeling that I had ever experienced.

I then reached over and returned the favor to my new friend. It was exciting to have John's hard dick in my hand. It seemed much harder than mine ever got. It arched up tight against his belly, and I had to pull it away in order to jack him off.

It wasn't long before he was arching his body up and shooting all over both of us. We then went swimming again to wash the jism off.

That was the start of our many happy experiences together. We soon included his older brother, Bob, who was my age, and some other friends into our little parties. We would all gather at one of our houses where it was safe, and strip naked and swim and jack each other off. We all enjoyed watching each other shoot off, and had all the normal contests and things.

Once when John, Bob, and I were alone, I sucked them off. Although they enjoyed it, they wouldn't reciprocate because they said it was queer. We fooled around for a couple of years until we started high school. Then they decided we were too old for that kind of stuff and started chasing girls to hold up their images. I didn't agree with their decision. I continued to have many more good times with other boys after that, although with some discretion, because I also had to hold up that macho image to fit into the high school crowd. I will save the stories of those other good times for another letter.

–Dallas, TX

Walter

*R*ecently I came across your magazine and enjoyed it thoroughly. I thought I would send you an experience that happened when I was younger.

I was out of school and entering college when I realized I would have to get a part-time job to make ends meet. My friends suggested I look in the school paper. The usual stuff was available, like hamburger joints, car washes and generally boring jobs. Then to my surprise I saw an ad for male models in the art department.

Curious, I applied for the job. I am not a Burt Reynolds or anything, but I was in great physical shape for eighteen – six feet one, slim and fairly muscular, with sandy blond hair and brown eyes. During the initial interview the lady asked if I had ever posed nude before. Of course I had not, but I was not ashamed of my body and told her so. She seemed interested and asked me to come by the next night and to be prepared to bare it for some other teachers.

That night I had to whack off a couple of times just thinking about it. Showing my body turned me on.

I showed up at seven, and was led into a room with two men and two women teachers. The older teacher instructed me to go in the large closet, remove my clothing and return. Quickly I did so, but it took a few minutes for my hard-on to subside. Eagerly I strolled in, each teacher closely examined me. Turn this way and that. Stand here. Bend there. The younger man took a Polaroid of me and I was hired.

My first job was for the senior students. I sat real turned on and completely naked for close to three hours. Twice, to my embarrassment, I got a hard-on and had to leave until it went down. After class, the teacher gave me a twenty-five dollar voucher and I started to my car. As I got to my car, I saw that I had a flat tire and realized there was no spare.

Walking towards the main gate one of the guys in the class stopped and offered me a ride home. He started casually making comments about what a great body I had, and that I held myself well. Then, as we approached my street, he confessed he wanted to blow me. I was startled. I had fooled around with boys when I was thirteen, but had not considered doing it again. That was until then.

My adrenaline was still pumping from fulfilling my fantasy in front of the students, so I said sure. We rode to his apartment and went in. He told me to get comfortable. We quickly stripped and I found him to be a turn-on.

He led me into the bedroom and lay me across the bed. Slipping into a jockstrap, he began licking my swollen cock, then tonguing my balls. This guy sure was good. He soon got to my nipples and chest, gently tonguing and nibbling.

He brought me to the edge of a climax two or three times, and then started licking my anus. Oh, shit! I'd never had anyone do this before. I was completely lost in the moment, and really did not feel it when he slipped a finger up me. I was so relaxed as he massaged my sphincter with lubricant and one finger, then two fingers.

It was then that I protested. Changing his tone, he abruptly prevented me from getting up. I struggled but to no avail. He pushed the head of his cock up in me. I bit the pillow as he maneuvered his seven inches to the hilt. Then in rabbit-like motions, he ravaged my sore, aching ass.

My first thought was fear and outrage, but dammit I was getting real turned on. Being butt-fucked by this guy was filling some primal need in me. As he pumped off, I exploded my cum all over the sheets and my belly. Wow, what an experience. I will always recall the night I had a man up my ass. It's always good for jerk-off sessions. Since then, I have been pro-positioned lots, but I just freak out and can't do it. Maybe someday I'll get it up my ass like before. I just wish I could go through it again.

—*Grapevine, TX*

Interstate Trucker Gets His

I 'm a trucker and so I'm away a lot. My wife likes me to get sex off guys while I'm out on the road so I can tell her about it when I get back home. She gets real hot and we fuck or she sucks my dick off while I tell her about the different guys who sucked my dick or I fucked up the ass while I was on the road.

At first I thought she was crazy for wanting me to fuck around with guys. I wondered if she wanted me to do it to keep me away from other women. But I found out she really likes to hear about guys screwing around together. Weird, huh? Well, I found out a long time ago sex is where you find it and before I got married to her I got sex off women and men so I already knew the ropes about getting sex off guys.

Don't get me wrong. When I go with another guy for sex I'm always the man and my dick is the one that gets the action. It ain't hard to find a guy that will take me on. 'Cause I'm a trucker helps, I guess. And having a big ol' dick like mine helps also. The best place is any rest room along the interstate. There are other good places, too.

Sometimes the guy that wants my dick will just come out and ask me for it. When I'm in a john taking a piss, I can tell if a guy is interested in getting my dick. If he is interested and wants it he will keep looking over at it. If I have the time and I'm wanting some sex when this happens, I make it real easy for the guy to see my dick and if he keeps on looking at it I get up about half hard so he can really see it and see how much I got.

When he says he wants it, we mostly go to my sleeper. Sometimes the guy will get a motel room or have a camper or something like that. I like that 'cause we can take our clothes off and get some hard sex. In the sleeper, if I'm just going to get a blowjob from the guy, I make him keep his clothes on. But if I'm going to fuck him up his ass I make him take his clothes off so he can get his legs real wide apart and up in the air so I can get all my big dick up inside his asshole. Most guys that like taking dick up their ass like getting it pushed in deep and want to take their clothes off so they can get wide open for it.

I keep Vaseline in my sleeper to put on my dick for fucking guys in the ass. It works best. I tried spit but it ain't slick enough; it's too hard getting my cock head pushed in. Vaseline works real good 'cause it is slick enough so I can push my dick head right in and it doesn't hurt my dick so much or the guy that is getting it in his ass, either. And it is a lot faster too 'cause I don't have to waste a lot of time getting the guy's asshole to open up for my dick.

I don't know which I like best, fucking a guy up his asshole or having him suck my dick. A tight asshole wrapped around my dick feels real good. But a hot sucking mouth with a hard tongue is a nice place to shoot my cum, especially if the guy sucking my dick knows how to take it down his throat when I get ready to cum. That is really good sex, but not too many guys know how to do that good.

So this is what I do when I get back home. I don't mind doing it for her. She gets so hot she just about fucks me out so sometimes I don't want any sex for two or three days when I go back out on the road. It is what she wants me to do and I do it to please her, so it works good for us. I like to see pictures of two women doing it so I guess women get hot when two men do it to each other.

Initiation Rites

I greatly enjoyed reading the article on hazing and initiations in the Spring issue of *FirstHand*. This letter is to describe my experiences in that area.

Eight years ago I was a senior at a Midwestern college. The fraternity I belonged to was initiating five pledges from the freshman class to join the eighteen upperclass brothers.

The initiation began with the pledges stripping for our inspection. Then each was shaved clean of all hair from the neck down. Groins, chest, and armpits were all bared. The pledges then underwent individual hazings. And what happened next is what really turned me on.

Four of the pledges were herded into a room on the second floor of the frat house leaving behind a guy named Bob. Bob was huge for an eighteen-year-old. He stood six-four and weighed in with two-hundred and forty pounds of muscle. The pledgemaster planned something special for Bob since the traditional paddling would be as effective as a flyswatter on an elephant.

There was a long, heavy oak table in the main room of the house and the pledgemaster told Bob to lie face up on it. Wide leather belts were strapped at Bob's ankles and wrists to hold him securely to the table. Despite his humiliating position, he seemed sure of his toughness. That soon changed.

The pledgemaster brought out four long, soft feathers. He gave one each to two other brothers, gave one to me, and kept one for himself. When Bob, tied and unable to move, saw the feathers a little bit of the arrogance left his eyes. The rest of the brothers settled themselves around the room to watch the spectacle.

As we had planned, the pledgemaster stood by Bob's left foot, I stood by his right foot and each of the other two hazers stood at the sides of the table. The pledgemaster explained that what went on in a fraternity was private business and we were going to test him to see if he could keep his mouth shut. No matter what we did, he was not allowed to make a sound.

The four of us used our feathers to tickle Bob. At his feet, the pledgemaster and I ran the soft feathers along Bob's soles, while the other brothers tickled him along his ribs and into his armpits. For a few seconds, our helpless victim was able to bite his lips and keep silent, but before a minute had gone by giggles were pouring out of him. Soon he was heaving with uncontrollable laughter. We relentlessly stroked his body with the feathers, running them between his toes. Bob was howling and trying to twist away from the torture, but the belts held him. There was nothing he could do but take it. Before long, he had forgotten about the order to say nothing and was begging us to quit.

We wouldn't. We started dragging the quill end of the feathers over his feet, which seemed to tickle even worse. The other two tormentors worked on the sensitive skin of his belly and neck.

We had been going over Bob for twenty minutes and our victim was in a bad state. His skin shone with sweat and tears were running down the sides of his face. He could barely catch his breath, but we didn't let up. Suddenly, Bob gave a shout and an arc of piss shot out from the tip of his cock. We were all stunned for a second and stopped tickling him. As soon as we did, he regained control of himself and stopped pissing. Well, now we really went after him – purposely tickling him to force him to drain his bladder.

When Bob was empty, we freed our poor, naked victim. He was beet red with shame and stimulation, dripping with sweat and his own piss. His knees almost buckled when he stood and we had to help him to a chair.

As for me, I was more turned on than I had ever been. For some reason this scene had really hit a nerve and I would have loved to give the other four pledges a dose of the same treatment. Sadly, other plans had been made.

Since that night, though, the idea of tying and tickling a helpless guy has been always on my mind. I've been able to persuade a few submissive men to undergo such an ordeal, although it doesn't happen nearly as often as I'd like. The whole scene, when combined with regular sex play, is electric.

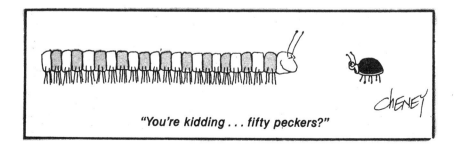

"You're kidding . . . fifty peckers?"

"I Wear Panties Under My Shorts"

I am a twenty-three-year-old, black bi-male who resides in the suburbs of a large city. One hot evening, I was sitting around (with my air conditioning on the blink), trying to think of a way to beat the heat.

I finally decided that I would borrow one of the neighbor's kid's bicycles and cruise through a nearby park. I got dressed in my jogging shorts, tennis shoes, etc. (by the way, I normally wear panties under my shorts) and went to borrow the bicycle. It was one of those dirt bikes with the banana seat and high handlebars.

After about fifteen minutes of riding in the park, I noticed a white fellow sitting on the side of the road. He couldn't have been any more than eighteen years old and had a very discouraged look on his face. I guess it was out of curiosity that I pulled over and stopped by him.

After asking him if there was anything wrong, he informed me that he was new to the area, he and his girlfriend had an argument, and she left him stranded in the park. While he was talking I could tell that he was stoned on pot and alcohol. Feeling sorry, I offered to ride him up to the nearest bus stop and direct him to where he was going. He accepted my offer and said that he had to take a leak first.

The next thing I knew, he was standing and swaying on the curb, pissing, apparently too high to care if anyone saw him or not. As his yellow stream hit the street, I couldn't help but notice that for a white guy, he was pretty well hung. Even at a state of semi-erection, it looked to be at least six or seven inches. I fought the sudden rush through my body. He finally finished and climbed on the rear of the bicycle.

With him holding me around my waist, I pushed off, pedaling up the street. He was no help at all as I tried to balance the two of us on the bike. I had come to a slight incline and had to stand while pedaling. The bike was wobbling wildly, and all of a sudden I lost control. We both went down on the concrete.

Neither of us were hurt but I noticed that I had ripped the seat of my shorts. Before I could cover the rip, he noticed my panties underneath and burst out in laughter. I tried to explain to him that panties were more comfortable for me, but he kept insisting that I was gay and should give him a blowjob. I refused and was about to leave him there when he grabbed my arm and apologized. He told me that he still would appreciate a ride.

Again feeling sorry for him, I allowed him to get back on the bike. We were now over the incline and coasting down the street. We weren't saying too much but I could feel his prick start to grow against my back. Trying to ignore it, I started getting an erection also.

I began to think about taking him up on his offer of giving him some head. I couldn't believe how big his cock felt on my backside. I wasn't going to make the first move though. Then all of a sudden he began pressing harder against me, apparently trying to get me to respond to his hard prick. Finally I thought, what the hell, and pulled the bike over and asked him what he was trying to do. He told me that the sight of my panties had excited him so much that he couldn't help but get a hard-on. He then offered me twenty dollars if I would allow him to masturbate while looking at me in my panties. "Twenty dollars," I thought. What can I lose? We pulled the bike behind some bushes and while I lowered my shorts, he unzipped his pants and pulled out his long, thick cock. I stood there watching him begin to pull and jerk on all that meat. Unable to take it any longer, I walked over to him and began rubbing the nylon material of my panties over the head of his cock. He moaned, and I dropped to my knees and took his now dripping cock into my mouth while he was still jerking off. He was just about to cum when he pulled away and suggested that we try something different. Curious and anxious, I asked what.

He pulled me up, turned me around and tore a hole in my panties. "Pull your shorts up," he said. Then he went and got on the bike with his cock sticking straight up. He told me to come and sit on it. I got on the bike in front of him as he carefully passed his cock through the holes in my shorts and panties. He was now lubricating the opening of my anus with his pre-cum and slowly pushing it in as I sat down. Boy, he was big, but the pain slowly subsided.

We rested for a while, then he told me to begin riding. I rode back onto the street and felt his cock go into me deeper and deeper with each movement I made. As my legs went up and down on the pedal, his cock would go in and out of my anus. The feeling was incredible, and I started pedaling harder trying to get more of him inside of me. We exited the park in this manner into the traffic. No one even knew what we were doing as we passed by many people. It looked as though we were just riding double.

There were some pretty foxy-looking women walking the streets and as we passed them he would comment on how he pretended that his cock was up their cunts. I would imagine how they would feel.

Finally, I felt him swell even larger. Unable to keep the bike in a straight line, I managed to steer into a parking lot. I knew he was about to shoot his load into me, so I stopped the bike between two parked cars and leaned forward over the handlebars. He began pumping into me wildly as I moaned and groaned with intense pleasure. Just as I had spread my legs wider, preparing for his climax, some women came into the garage to get their car. They noticed us just as my rider began to shoot cum deep into my bowels. Seeing the women watch me getting screwed also set off my orgasm, and I began shooting my load, all in my panties.

We cleaned up as best we could, and I directed him to the nearest bus stop. I rode home and took a nice long hot bath to soothe my well-stretched, sore ass.

There are a few things I forgot though: his name, to give him my phone number, and to get my *twenty dollars!*

—*St. Louis, Missouri*

"Sir Henry, some of the other knights have been complaining about your peculiar jousting habits..."

Samurai Lust

B Y   A L A N   A R T H U R

*W*hile in Tokyo on business, I reactivated an old friendship with Tomiyoshi, a twenty-eight-year-old, tallish, awfully attractive, suited hunk with soulful eyes and a naughty sense of humor. I had originally met him at an East Coast business conference, and we had hit it off socially.

We connected at a Tokyo beer hall, and after a few drinks, Tomiyoshi revealed that he'd never had anal sex. I kept that in mind, although he hadn't said it as a come-on. He just was very frank for a Japanese. Then Tomiyoshi asked me what I wanted to do for the evening.

My first thought was the male communal baths, and since my non-westernized hotel had one, we were in it at seven p.m. It took time to acclimatize myself to the scalding water. The businessmen beside me looked younger than middle-aged, and some were in their twenties. Most had large pubic bushes with unaroused peckers. Still, I enjoyed watching, disconcerting only a few. Tomiyoshi had already told me, "In Buddhism, we do not have the concept of sexual sin, and homosexuality is a bodily function that some men crave and others don't. So don't worry as long as you are relatively discreet."

When I was sweating like a pig, I got out and headed for the hall. Then I went to the lockers to have a cigarette, still nude but half-erect from the heat. When I entered, three Japanese youths (hotel employees?) were standing outside the door, chatting and smiling. Real cute stuff. One of them opened the door, saw me, and quickly shut the door. I continued smoking, and when the cigarette was almost to an end, the same boy came in nervously and walked to the end of the room, sneaking a glance at my cock. He obviously was there to see a western, uncut penis.

He went out, and I heard loud whispering. I was hoping he might come back and bring his friends.

Putting my butt out, I wrapped a towel around my hips and peered out the door. The boys were shocked to see me, and when I smiled, one rushed off. The other two were embarrassed as though I'd understood what they were saying. Trying my luck, I offered, "Why don't you enjoy the bath?" This caused the second friend to bow and depart hurriedly. The boy who'd spied on my cock did come in hesitantly, gesturing that he spoke no English.

Nonchalantly, I let the towel slip off, then took my cock in hand, getting it hard in seconds. (In Japan, men sometimes pee on the street, so penises aren't shocking mysteries, except for western men's.) To make a long story short, the youth wasn't willing to do anything in the locker room—I couldn't blame him. So I wrote my room number down on some paper. An hour later, he arrived and shyly sucked my cock. I shot into his mouth shortly, and he spit my cum out politely, then bowed and left. I didn't get a chance to sample his but I'd known from Tomiyoshi that to have offered the boy money would have been very demeaning, so I didn't chase after him with a bill. I told Tomiyoshi what happened, and said I hoped that this was the first of many such experiences.

He suddenly asked, somewhat abruptly, "Do you want to see what you call gay Japan?" I nodded eagerly. "I am so sorry. I had thought you want to see tourists' Japan. Cultural Japan."

"I do, definitely. But I'm here a whole week, and other than you, to be honest, I've never known a Japanese person, let alone a gay Japanese man."

Eventually, Tomiyoshi would carefully, gently (fortunately, he wasn't all that gentle in bed) explain that he did not consider himself "homosexual" or "heterosexual," but "a loving man." He wasn't one for labels. He smiled and said, "I will be your host for this cultural, sexy tour, my friend."

That night, Tomiyoshi took me to Roppongi, a lively entertainment district full of nightclubs. We sampled two: drinks at *Cleopatra*, a gay bar, and then on to *Sugar Boy*, which appeared to be a popular bar with pretty, attentive hostesses. Tomiyoshi and I talked of the differences in our cultures and their beliefs, while noticing a particular hostess eyeing me. She was diminutive, feminine, hiding her smile behind beautifully manicured hands. I could see her in a geisha costume. Finally, I asked my friend, "She seems interested in, or amused by, me. Am I supposed to do something not to be rude?"

"Do you like to dance with her?" he asked. I did and I did.

"My name is Sachiko," she said with a Lauren Bacall–like grit to her voice. We danced two numbers: the latest disco hit, and a slow one I recognized but didn't know the name of. Then, in the middle of the dance, her fingertips brushed my penis as if by accident. But they returned, jabbing into me, while she looked me directly in the eye. I quickly whispered, "I'm sorry, I'm not interested in that."

She smiled. "You already have a boyfriend?"

Only then did I realize the "hostesses" were males, and this was also a gay bar. Why hadn't Tomiyoshi mentioned it? "I assumed you knew," he said. "You did not say you liked the girls, so I assumed you didn't like feminine boys. I prefer male men, too."

Since Tomiyoshi lived on the outskirts of the world's biggest city, we wound up at my place. However, he dragged himself out of bed, firmly declining to stay the night. I hated to let him go. I admired his molded ass and remarked, "You're big for a Japanese, aren't you?" He didn't take my meaning, and said, "Yes, yes. I play on company's basketball team."

The next day, Tomiyoshi asked, "Do you want to see unusual geisha?"

I nodded yes, and we headed for Akasaka, one of the city's geisha districts. On the way, he carefully explained about *male* geisha for *women*. Like our own male hookers for women, they are predominantly bisexual, but tamer. These young men mostly chatted with the affluent, bored housewives (Japan has very few businesswomen) and sometimes allowed them to cop a feel.

It was early when we arrived at the house where three male geisha lived. Tomiyoshi led the way, and we went into a small room to undress. We then went to another room and put our cocks through silk-lined glory-holes. Within seconds, I felt a warm, moist mouth around mine.

"Male?" I asked Tomiyoshi.

"Hai," he nodded. Then, by his abstracted expression, I could see Tomiyoshi's big, juicy prick had found its own temporary home. He looked up towards the ceiling, eyes half shut. I watched my sexy friend, placing my hand on his butt. I eventually moved to take it off, but Tomiyoshi whipped his hand on top of mine, pressing it.

"I'll have orgasm," he moaned-whispered in my direction. I pushed my index finger into his ass. Then, as I heard him utter a guttural cry, I pushed it further up his ass and felt the slippery inside of my latest lover. My finger still in him, I had my own ejaculation; the mouth at the other end knew what to do, and took all of me as far down as possible, not releasing for over a minute. I nearly fell backwards, but Tomiyoshi caught me and gave me a playful kiss on the lips.

Now what? We showered, then entered the bathing room, where we descended into a scalding hot tub, the two of us alone.

"In half an hour, twenty men will come here," Tomiyoshi informed me.

I asked, "So why the glory-holes, if these were males catering to women?"

"That is public image and shocking to Japanese men. But for practicalness, men who like oral sex done come here before or after official hours."

"Why don't the young men suck on us without the partition?"

"It is considered privacy. For us and for them. They do not acknowledge themselves as homosexual prostitutes."

After the enervating soak which had followed our enervating early-morning blowjobs, Tomiyoshi and I fell onto massage tables in the next room. (The place was like a rabbit warren of small rooms, each differently scented.) There we were alternately pummeled and cuddled by cute Japanese youths (our suckers?), and I started into a pleasant, if violent, daydream. When we were through, the place was alive with noise—the twenty had arrived and were probably in the process of being glory-holed.

Another morning, Tomiyoshi took me to the *Acropolis*, Tokyo's first all-gay massage parlor. It was housed in the businessmen's Rasshington Palace Hotel, located in the youth-oriented Shinjuku section. (Like many gay places, it features— at night—a purple light outside.) You actually did get massage here, but with a difference: the young man got on top of you either wearing a bikini or nothing, depending on whether you were puritanical westerner or sane. The masseur then used himself as a towel and fingers.

Mine had doused himself in aromatic strawberry oil, and began slithering above and to the side of me like a sexy boa constrictor. I became oily too, and we'd switch without friction, working our way up and down and around each other.

The strawberry scent wasn't too strong, and he assured me, "It not poison. You can lick-eat." He certainly used his mouth. On places where the sun doesn't shine, too.

Besides the sexual moves and the eating my masseur did on various parts of my anatomy, he did give me a fair amount of stimulating, therapeutic massage. If he was sweating, I couldn't tell through the oil, but he more than earned the $60 fee for the sixty minutes—through most of which we were both hard-as-bricks.

One evening, in Shinjuku, we played pachinko and several video games for a couple of hours. Then Tomiyoshi mentioned he knew a "family brothello." By that time, he'd ascertained that I was fond of getting rimmed. "I have specialty taste, too," he smiled mysteriously. So we went inside an undistinguished building, up the elevator, and my pal escorted me into a cubicle without a bed. It had a thick mat instead.

"Wait. He comes to you."

In a minute or less, a man, aged anywhere twenty to forty years old, walked in with a black mask on his face. He placed a timer at the edge of the matted floor, set for 15 minutes. He had on a black bikini with zippers at the sides. Lying down on his back, silently, he then motioned for me to sit on his face, once my clothes were off.

Before this experience I'd have said fifteen minutes of rimming would leave me bored and/or sore. No way. It was heavenly. Like a leech, this masked man (I never saw his face) sucked his mouth onto and into my ass. Instantly he made strange sounds, sending oddly sensual feelings up my ass and shivers through my spine. The man had made an art out of this kind of pleasure. And it wasn't just a job to him! He must have been a fetishist, because he came twice during the session, playing with himself after breaking away his bikini.

Afterwards, I asked Tomiyoshi, "Is this what the man does for a living?"

For once, he allowed himself to laugh at my expense. "No. The man is a colleague of mine, though I know not which name. Men from our company (which was a multinational) come here. The women not allowed to do this. But men come to have the sex they want, to give, to get the pleasure. They are paid something, but minimal, for maintenance here."

After I got over that—imagine a bordello staffed by IBM-type execs and workers during their off-hours—I asked Tomiyoshi what he'd done. "I was greedy," he blushed. "Two men. One sucks my toes. One kisses my testes. While I masturbated more than once."

I asked Tomiyoshi to describe it in more detail. But though he was frank with his language at times, especially with references to my cock, he turned crimson while trying to explain why he enjoyed having his balls kissed and licked. I didn't push him, and we had lunch at a crowded fast-food restaurant.

In a cab with a non-English-speaking driver, I reminded my friend that the first time we'd hurriedly had sex in the States, sixty-nining till we each came. I'd tried to grab hold of his balls, but he'd squirmed and avoided me. Tomiyoshi withheld comment.

That night in Tokyo, we indulged in more oral sex and a lot of petting, but when I reached for his scrotum, he grimaced. He seemed to have an aversion to having his balls held. Finally, Tomiyoshi explained that when he was a child, his sadistic older brother would punish him for imaginary offenses by pulling on his balls, holding them and tugging until Tomiyoshi reluctantly squealed with pain or, twice, blacked out.

"But if a man puts his mouth on my testes, he is honoring them and me. It is sexy, and pleasure-filled." Again, his frankness was impersonal, not to be taken as a tease or a suggestion.

That night, Tomiyoshi couldn't come to my hotel room due to a family engagement. But on the following night I asked him and got him to promise to stay till morning. It was a big hotel, so who would notice? Besides, if sex weren't a sin, what was there to worry about?"

"But you are *gaijin*" (a foreigner), he said, apologizing for the xenophobia that both our countries are afflicted with.

First we cuddled under the sheets, and Tomiyoshi again covered my face with kisses. His eyes were fantastic to look into, large and soulful. I kissed his almost smooth, well-muscled chest, noting his tapering waist and the trail of hairs that led to his generous pubic bush. Throwing the covers off, I rubbed my nose in his bush; he giggled in that unfeminine way Japanese men have. Then I put my lips to his balls, which were roundly inviting. I licked the shaft of his cock, pushed it towards his stomach with my lips, then concentrated on his balls.

"It's all right to touch," he said, indicating he didn't have a phobia about it. So I pushed each testicle into my mouth, easily getting both in. Then I swirled my tongue over them, inhaling their musky aroma while listening for my lover's soothing groans of pleasure.

I felt such a strong affection, I wanted to postpone my own release until later . . . until after I'd given Tomiyoshi every erotic experience I could think of. I sucked on his long, meaty horn of plenty until it almost came. Then I bit gently on the insides of his thighs, working my way down to his well-shaped feet. I put his big toe in my mouth and sucked it seductively. Then I licked the ball of his perfectly clean foot and tickled the undersides of his toes with my tongue, chewing some more. He did the same to me, which gave him obvious pleasure.

But Tomiyoshi had never been fucked or so he said. To rid him of this sad fact, I polished his sphincter with my tongue and inserted a finger.

"Did you like when I did it at the geisha house?" I asked.

He nodded, so I put two in, then three. I knew he was ready for me. Sliding in slowly, I grabbed this sweet hunk to me and pummeled his virgin ass with my eager cock. I knew I'd come in a minute or two after all that stimulation, and I did, but I kept pumping for a good fifteen minutes until I came again. My Oriental paramour loved it, making sure we fucked the next morning and early afternoon. We finally went out to eat, giving the frustrated maid time to make my bed, but only after Tomi-yoshi swore he'd bring his willing buns to San Francisco within the coming year.

"Wow, Maurice... You really are a head waiter!"

Instant Erections In High School

I would like to share with you and your readers my first gay sex experience.

I am from a very large, happy and healthy Italian family. Growing up with several brothers and sisters gave me ample opportunity to play some of the usual "sex games" of young children. My father is a doctor, and we often used some of his equipment in playing "doctor." When I was in the sixth grade, I got my private bedroom, and from that time on there was no more touching, comparing, or grabbing.

I was very shy about my body, both clothed and nude. I hit puberty the summer between fifth and sixth grade. I started sprouting hair everywhere. My three older brothers still have very smooth skin and virtually hairless bodies. Occasionally, they teased me about having more hair on one arm than the three of them had on all six legs. I became self-conscious about this and wore long-sleeved shirts in even the hottest weather. I never wore cut-offs or shorts.

In seventh grade, I began gym class, so I had to strip in the locker room with my classmates. I don't recall anyone being cruel, but I received a lot of teasing about looking like a fly with all my hair. Although I did not like the teasing, I did enjoy the attention. I was looked upon as being so much more mature and having all the answers about growing up sexually. There was a group of guys that used to jerk off in the locker room occasionally during the lunch hour. I had heard from others that it was a lot of jerking, but they were too young to get off. Part of me wanted to get in on this to "show them," but a part of me was afraid of the idea. One day I was walking through the corridor near the locker room when about five of them were coming along. They invited me to join them, and I said yes, mainly because I thought they might think me a sissy if I said no.

As long as I can remember I seem to have had a hard-on most of every day. Just the slightest thought of anything sexual, and I'd get an instant erection. All through junior and senior high, I got an erection every time I put on my jockstrap for gym class, football, wrestling, and baseball. As I look back I am surprised that I wasn't harassed about that. All the guys that had lockers near mine made comments to me, but those comments were more out of curiosity or expressions of them being impressed by the speed of the rise and the size of my penis. In seventh grade, I had close to seven inches hard. I haven't added any length since then.

When we entered the locker room for my first cirle jerk, I had a hard-on before the door was shut. We went to the back where one of the guys threw soiled towels from the laundry cart on the floor. We stood around the pile of towels, and everyone quickly unzipped, dropped their pants to the floor, and started pumping away. Because I was new to the group and was not even used to private masturbation, I was planning to stay slightly behind the others so I would first see what they did and then follow. I was going to allow some of them to come first to avid attention. But as soon as I dropped my pants, my hard-on sprang out and up, throbbing like it might be too big for the skin. Everyone else was still soft and working at getting their meat pumped up. I was now the center of attention. I could not just stand there while they were trying to catch up, so I grabbed my cock and tried to gently stroke it. In about two and a half srokes, I shot a huge load across the pile of towels and between two of the fellows across the circle.

I was terribly embarrassed until I realized that they were all impressed. (In seventh grade, nobody seems interested in prolonging sex.) I really did not know what was expected of me, so I awkwardly waited while they all commented and continued to pump furiously. I was still very hard, so I began pumping again. This time I was able to do a lot more pumping. A couple of the fellows came, but their cum was little in quantity and more of a clear and watery fluid. I came again, not with such volume as the first, but it was a thick and rich load. Three or four of the guys did not come at all but simply got tired of pumping. The towels were quickly tossed back into the basket, and we got ourselves pulled together.

By noon the next day most of the guys in the class had heard about my virility. The story was exaggerated, stating that I had shot quarts of cum three times. I found all this very embarrassing as sex did not predominate my life. I was even more embarrassed when I discovered that most of the girls in my class had heard about what an "animal" I was. Our school and town were small, and it does not take long for that kind of hot stuff to spread through the school and beyond.

Through my first ten years of school, I was quite shy. I was always polite and could converse with others, but did not like to draw attention to myself in any way. Our family was very open and honest about sex and responsible sexual behavior.

As I mentioned before, I did very little masturbating. It was not because I was ever led to believe that it was evil; it was that I did not find much pleasure in it. I guess I tried it a half-dozen times in my life. The first couple were just so I would know what others were talking about. The other times were to see if it got better as I grew up. (I still don't masturbate as I have some wonderful wet dreams about once a week. I wouldn't do anything to miss them.)

I did not like the attention or the pressure to show my stuff for the rest of the class. The "easy" girls came on pretty strong toward me. They were people I did not like, and I was not about to give them my virginal penis so they could report back to the rest of the girls. By the next school year, I guess the excitement was gone. Most of the rest of the guys had hit puberty, and they were all into their own methods of dealing with the event.

The rest of my high school career was quite uneventful. I was very active in sports, drama, band, and several clubs. It was not until my junior year that I was willing to take any positions of leadership in these activities. I started dating as a junior and found girls to be my most exciting discovery. A lot of them wanted to get laid by the captain of the wrestling team (I looked great in my singlet) and Macbeth. I was happy to make them happy. I did not date a lot but for two years I screwed a couple of times a week with my regulars. I won't say that they were deep and meaningful relationships, but there was more to them than fucking.

When I entered college, I decided to abstain from sex and dating so that I could give full attention to my academic work. My parents were against financing my college education, so I had to work my way through college. I did not want my hard-earned money to be wasted. Getting along without sex was unusual but I found it to be a challenge. I was busy enough with a full load of courses, a twenty-four-a-week job, wrestling, and other extra-curricular activities, not to be able to give thought to what I was missing.

As part of working toward a degree in English, I tutored students in the area of composition and communication skills. In this work I came to kow many fine students that were struggling with a variety of college courses.

Through this tutorial service I came to know Stan. I was a junior and Stan a freshman. He was a tall and quite athletic black student. I came to discover that he was a very warm and outgoing young man, although he felt a good deal of insecurity in that there were only four black men on the campus. Along with my specific task of helping him in the area of composition,

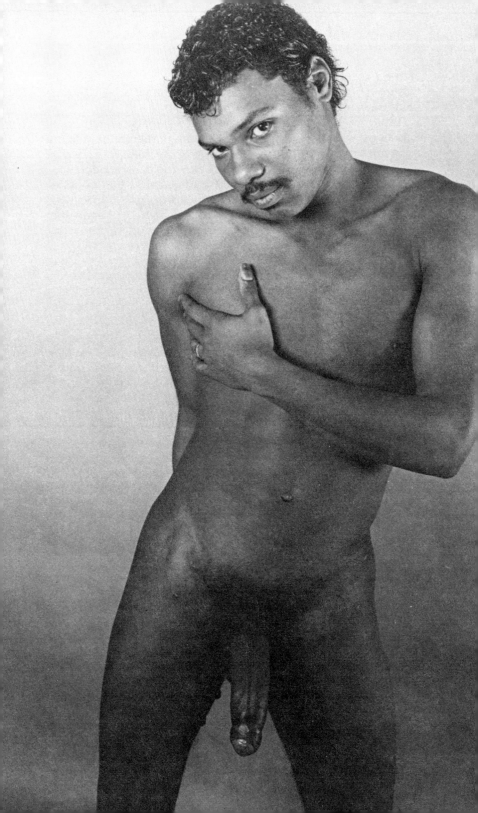

I tried to encourage him to become more active in events around the college. In the course of the year, he began to come out of his shell.

I tutored Stan about twice a week at 9 p.m. We would spend about an hour each time developing an understanding about usage of grammar and literary style. Occasionally, we would end up at the student union for a Coke and conversation.

One evening, just before the winter break, I had gone ice skating with a couple of guys from the dorm. Although I stayed in good physical shape and was very active, I found that skating used muscles that weren't used in handball and wrestling. I returned to the dorm tired and sore. I dragged myself out of several layers of winter clothing, wrapped a towel around my waist, grabbed the soap and shampoo, and headed for the dorm showers. I took a long hot shower in an attempt to warm up and relax the muscles that were tightening up in the back of my upper legs. While in the shower, I decided to go right to bed and get up a couple of hours earlier than usual to study before I went to work at 5 a.m. I walked back to my room to find Stan sitting there waiting for me. I had forgotten that I was scheduled to work with him that night. I told him about the skating and how tired and sore I was. He suggested that I stretch out on the bed and he would give me a rubdown while I read over a paper he had written for sociology. I took him up on the offer and lay face down on the bed and picked up his composition.

As he started massaging my neck and shoulders, I asked a few general questions about the paper. We both fell silent as I began reading through the script. I really did not pay all that much attention to the massage as I have had many of them from various trainers throughout high school and college. I did notice that his hands seemed very large and were strong and firm. As I read, he worked the muscles of my back down to my waist. The movements of his hands combined a deep massage and a gentle caress.

After spending a good amount of time on my back, Stan undid my towel and calmly continued to rub my ass cheeks and my legs. He worked his fingers deeply into the muscles of my legs. I commented about how good that felt and about him assisting the wrestling team trainer. He said something about getting all my muscles to relax so the ones in the legs could. He continued to work on down the legs to my ankles and feet. He gently took each foot and concentrated on massaging the soles. Although there was still a slight soreness in my legs, I was feeling very relaxed. I had completed reading the paper, but was too mellow to start discussing possible improvements. I put my head down and closed my eyes.

Stan continued to work up and down my legs, occasionally massaging my buns and then up and down my back again. Whenever he worked on the insides of the upper part of my legs, his fingers gently worked on the underside of my balls. Occasionally, he touched my cock that was pointed toward my feet. As usual it was rock hard. This did not concern me, as every time I have had a rubdown I have had an erection. The trainers seemed to ignore or at least expect this reaction from me. None of them ever tried to do anything with it, and I really did not expect them to.

Stan continued his attention to the entirety of my backside and suggested that I roll over. At the same time, he gently rolled me over. My cock slapped hard against my abdomen, stretching to my navel. Stan seemed to ignore this and began a deep rub of my shoulders and chest. He worked hard on my pectoral muscles and then down my ribs and belly. His hands slid between my belly and cock and then around the groin area. He worked the outer thighs and down my legs. On the way back up, he concentrated more on the inner legs. His hands moved into my crotch and behind my balls. Although he covered a lot more area than others covered, he seemed very professional or businesslike about the whole thing. As his hands again came above my cock and across my belly, I felt his hands slide on the moisture of a small pool of pre-cum that had flowed into my navel. With one finger, he wiped the fluid out of the navel and began rubbing it across my abdomen. At first it made everything very slick, but it quickly dried from the heat of my body and became sticky.

Stan said something about seeing if there was any more and took my cock in his hand with his thumb on the bottom of the base of the tool. He drew his hand firmly up the length of the cock, forcing more of the shiny fluid into his hand. He did not spread it over my stomach but cupped his hand over the head of my penis and smoothed my pre-cum around the head and down the length of the shaft. He then firmly began to stroke my cock that was so hard it actually hurt. Within four or five strokes, I shot a great stream of cum that arched into the air, falling onto my face, my hair, and my chest. Several other bursts followed, soaking the front of me. Stan squeezed the remainder from my cock and began to firmly work my thick cum into my hairy chest and stomach.

I was somewhat embarrassed and confused as he continued

his silent massage. The room seemed to fill with the smell of my own cum. I had never realized that there was so much odor to the juice of passion. I loved the smell and inhaled deeply. I did not know what would happen or what I should do next. I was relieved when Stan said to relax while he cleaned me up. He soaked a washcloth in warm water from my sink and thoroughly washed off my stomach, chest, face and hair. Then he carefully dried me with a hand towel. I don't think my cock had become soft at all and was still pointing due north.

Stan then sat on the edge of the bed and gently stroked my chest and ran his fingertips down my belly and around my crotch. My cock jumped several times before he again took my cock in his hand. He then lowered his face on it to gently blow on my cock and balls. He inhaled my cock into his mouth that was much hotter than I expected. It was a feeling that I had never experienced. As his lips and tongue caressed my cock, it seemed too full. While he massaged my cock with his mouth, his hands roamed all over my body from head to toe. Much sooner than I wanted I came again, this time in his mouth. Although I am sure this second load was not as heavy as the first, I could feel numerous spurts and a lot of throbbing. Stan sucked every last drop from my cock and kissed it clean.

With his lips barely touching me, he kissed his way up my chest, lingering at my neck, and then gently but firmly kissed me full on the mouth. My lips parted, and his tongue moved inside, filling my mouth with the taste and odor of my own cum. I loved it and tried to clean all remains of it from Stan's mouth.

After several minutes of this very passionate kissing and probing, Stan moved his way back down to my crotch where my cock was softer but still quite erect. He licked, kissed, and sucked on my balls and ball sac. Again he slid my cock into his mouth, swallowing it to the base. He moved slowly up and down the shaft, turning his head from side to side. It was glorious as I could gradually feel myself getting harder again. This time climax was not so quick, so I had more time to enjoy the approach to a very long and deep climax. When I came I could feel my insides pushing and jerking. My balls had pulled themselves up so tight, they were causing a dull pain. I could tell that the cum was very thick and heavy. I really wanted to taste and drink it, but Stan was swallowing each shot as it came.

After Stan had sucked and licked me dry, he sat up and stared into my face for a few moments. Then he quickly kissed me, gathered up his papers, and left the room, saying that he would see me on Friday. As he left, I noticed that his cock seemed to extend half-way to his knee. I think that was the first crotch I ever noticed. It was the start of a life of careful crotch observing.

After Stan left, I remained stretched out on the bed wondering about all that had just transpired. I quickly drifted off to sleep until three o'clock when my alarm jolted me awake. Although not very much awake, I began addressing my studies for a couple of hours before work. I hurried off to where I cleaned an office building before it opened for business. All the while I was cleaning, I was thinking about Stan and how well he handled my body. I admitted to myself that I found the encounter exciting and enjoyable. I tried to think about what this would mean in my life, in my relationship with Stan, in my relationship with other men, and in my relationship with women. These concerns were also in my mind throughout the day of class work. I saw Stan twice in the halls and spoke. He seemed to react as he always did. I was concerned as to what I would say when he came for tutoring on Friday.

Friday night at 9 p.m., Stan showed up at my door. He walked in, dropped his books on my desk, and, as he took off his coat, said, "Let's get comfortable before we go to work." He quickly unbuttoned and removed a heavy flannel shirt he was wearing and helped me pull my sweater over my head.

He stripped himself in the manner one does in a locker room. He kicked off his shoes, dropped his pants, and stepped out of them. He wore no underwear. He remarked about my slowness and proceeded to pull off my shoes, socks, pants and undershorts. He helped me to my feet and held me in a strong embrace. Through all of this, I was trying to find a way to say that I thought we should talk about what had happened and what was happening. I was not really sure if I wanted it to continue. My major concern was whether or not this activity would fit into my well-planned life.

As Stan held me, I felt the heat of his body. He seemed surprisingly hot for just coming in from the cold. He eased his grip, holding my shoulders at arm's length. He looked deep into me and then drew me to him. The instant our lips touched, I melted into him, knowing that there was nothing I wanted to discuss at the moment. We kissed hard and deep while our hands roamed over each other's backs and butts. He lowered both of us to the bed, where he arranged me and told me to relax. He proceeded to kiss, lick, and nibble my face, neck, and shoulders. He turn his attention to my nipples, bathing them with his tongue. Gradually he nipped them and applied more pressure with his lips and tongue. I had not experienced this treatment before and was loving the ecstasy it produced. I was so excited I was writhing all over the bed, grabbing at his head to hold it tight to me. Suddenly I shot my load all over both of us. He caught a good amount of it in his armpit that was directly over me. Although I had ejaculated, I really had not climaxed. Stan was trying to lap up the cum as fast as he could. I was trying to get a taste of it from his armpit. I nearly went crazy as I gathered my cum and his manly odor into my mouth. I surprised myself when I did a reversal and pinned him to the bed, so that I could give him my full attention. I was in too much of a frenzy to want to spend any time at that point in caressing and kissing. I wanted a full mouth of cum, and I wanted it right away.

I aimed my head and mouth for the general direction of his cock. For the first time, I saw it in all its splendor. I was startled to see that it was nearly a foot long, thick and blacker than the rest of his body. I might have been frightened off if it had not been for the nice pearl of pre-cum nestled in the slit of that huge head.

I grabbed the base of his cock and hungrily lapped at the slit and its contents. The taste was milder than my cum, but very addicting. With no hesitation, I plunged his cock into my mouth and began to suck hard. I wanted all of the cock, but about half-way down the shaft the head hit the back of my throat. As I started to gag, I adjusted myself so that I could work on his balls with my right hand and his tits with my left. Sucking like crazy, I began to move my head up and down and in a circular manner, imitating his movements from two nights before.

I thought something must be wrong when Stan did not cum quickly. I was about to give up when he started to moan softly and thrust his hips up to meet me. I realized that he did not pop as quickly as I, but that it was going to happen. His moan turned to a low growl as he took my head in his hands to stop my motion. I did not understand this action until I felt his cock in my mouth suddenly expand and throb. It throbbed violently twice, and then my mouth quickly filled with hot cum as spurt after spurt shot into the back of my throat. I was trying to swallow, breathe, and hang on for dear life. I could not swallow fast enough, and some of the heavy, thick cum was escaping from my lips and running down his cock. What I was able to taste and swallow was rich and salty. It was stronger tasting and saltier than the couple of little tastes I had of my own. Squeezing his cock with my lips, I tried to draw every drop into my throat. I then began to lick up the cum that was at the base of his cock and in his tightly curled pubic hair. I licked and sucked all around his crotch, making sure that I did not miss a drop. I was kneeling beside him, looking down at his long, dark body. This was the first time that I really had the opportunity to give it visual attention.

Stan's cock softened quickly and was resting lazily over his left hip. His chest and stomach had a slight glow from the perspiration of excitement. His body was a rich black that revealed every muscle and vein. I thrilled to see the veins in his abdomen, thighs, and legs still pulsing quickly. I started moving my hands gently over his hard body. He drew me down to him and curled his arms around me in a gentle embrace. We lay there for several minutes not moving, just listening to each other's heartbeats. Stan sat up and stretched. He looked down at my cock that was still hard, grabbed it firmly, and said, "We've got some studying to do. Let's get that out of the way, and then I'm going to suck you until this thing can't stay hard any more."

That's just what we did. We quickly dressed and got to studying. I was not really able to concentrate on what the course material was, but Stan seemed to do very well. After about an hour, Stan snapped shut the books, reached over, and began to massage my cock through my jeans. He gave me a hungry grin as he felt my cock that had stayed hard all during our study time. His hand felt a wet spot on the denim, and his mouth went down to taste it. He started chewing on the fabric and on the head of my cock. I warned him that I could not take much of that stimulation. He pulled away, and we both stripped as quickly as possible.

I don't remember how many times I came that night. I do remember that it was the most exciting time I had ever had. I remember bringing Stan to climax a couple of times. He really seemed to be more interested in giving me all kinds of attention than having me reciprocate. In the course of the night, Stan must have massaged, sucked, licked, and nibbled every square inch of my body. He could not seem to get enough of my cock. He sucked me off at least a half-dozen times. Between climaxes, he sucked on my balls and gave my ass a great tongue washing. I had never been so stimulated in my life. After hours of this passionate sucking, kissing, nibbling, and licking, I finally reached the point when my cock began to soften. I recognized at that time that this was a first. My body and brain were being stimulated, and my cock was not responding. I felt happy and satisfied.

During my remaining time in college, I continued to tutor Stan, and we continued to have sex one night a week. I was still too disciplined to allow this new dimension of our relationship to interfere with all the activities and plans I had.

I knew from the time of our first sex together that I enjoyed sex with a man more than I had with any woman. Although the thought of sex with a woman is not repulsive to me, I simply have no desire to have sex with them any more.

The summer between my junior and senior years, I was not ready to come out of the closet and not aggressive enough to go hunting for men. I dated some women, because we were good friends, but I had no desire to be with them. Stan spent the summer in his hometown. We did not see each other nor did we write. I thought that he might not return in the fall, or if he did he might not be interested in me. I was more than pleased to find that when he came back, he was still very interested in me.

I have not seen Stan since graduation from college. Although we had what I considered to be great sex, we did not seem to have much else in common. There never was a bond between us.

I have been out of college for ten years now and have a good job that I greatly enjoy. I travel all over the country meeting and working with hundreds of people. Although I have many opportunities, I engage in sex only about once a month. Occasionally, the partners I choose are new ones, but usually I like to have sex with men that I have met over the past years. There are five guys that I meet in various cities in my travels that I have found to be mutually satisfying.

I know that there is a lot in the area of sex that I have not experienced. I don't find any desire to experience those aspects that are missing. I enjoy reading about group sex, discipline, and anal sex, but really have no desire to try them. Stan may have spoiled me. He gave me so much intense attention and affection. That is what I really look for and enjoy in sex now.

Although I don't have a hard-on as often as I did in high school and college, I still get one with the slightest suggestion. (My cock has been poking the bottom of my typing table all during this letter.) I still enjoy fantastic wet dreams about every four to five nights. My dream fantasies are well worth the messy bed linens.
                                                              —*Chicago, Illinois*

Ain't There No Virgins in West Virginia?

BY   KEITH   A.   HOLTZCLAW

C rossing the state line, I thought about the roadside sign proclaiming a welcome to: *Wild Wonderful West Virginia — Almost Heaven.* I knew leaving my city of over a million for a small mountain community would create major changes in my life. I also knew I couldn't pass on the opportunity to advance my career in hotel management through the position I had accepted at the ski resort. I hoped the crowded ski slopes would replace the lively bars for me, and the exhilaration of the fast-paced, white water rafting with virile, handsome guides would help me forget the ever-so-satisfying baths. With luck, the thrill and excitement of rock climbing with those strong deeply tanned legs in scant cutoffs scaling the rocks, and the forceful studs behind the wheel of powerful pickup trucks would keep my mind off the seedy bookstores. Crossing my fingers, I told myself I'd learn that a plug of chewing tobacco could replace Sunday morning quiche, and *Perrier* was not nearly as tasty as a cold *Moosehead.*

From my cabin in the woods it's a five-hour drive to the nearest gay bar. Hell, it's a sixty-mile drive each way just to conquer a *Big Mac* attack. However, all was not bad in this mountain hamlet of a few hundred country folk. Some of the best-looking, well-built hunks of gutsy male meat in the world flourish in these hills. Across the country, gay men spend fortunes at health clubs to have grueling workouts. Here the godlike bodies are a part of nature. Never before had I seen so many hot, sizzling studs in well-worn, snug-fitting jeans. What was beneath these uniforms were the subjects of my dreams.

After only three months in this wonderland, I was about to climb the walls. There was plenty of work to keep me busy, but with all the look-but-don't-touch merchandise around me, all I seemed to accomplish were endless hours of jacking off. I sought to fill my spare time with community activities, hoping to keep my mind off the sex I was doing without. I became a member of the volunteer fire department (VFD) and found myself working with some of the finest specimens of the community's male population. One of these rugged fire fighters became a friend.

Spencer, my age and single, had been out of the county only during the three years he spent in the Navy. He was a coal miner and also farmed several acres. Spencer drank beer like I did iced tea, but I never saw him drunk. He was six feet three inches tall, with jet black hair and a full beard that enhanced his rugged looks. His sparkling green eyes were captivating. Without ever having lifted a weight, he could have walked away with top honors in any body-building contest. I spent countless hours pounding the hell out of my meat thinking about this fantasy man come to life.

By this time I had learned that many of the local men felt queers served a purpose; some even boasted of having received a good blow job. Still I made every effort to conceal my sexual preferences.

In the late spring, Spencer asked if I wanted to do some fishing one night after a VFD meeting. Dry Fork River ran through his property and it was one of the most beautiful places I had ever seen. I didn't know anything about fishing, but agreed to go. I was surprised when he told me to get in the jeep so we could get started. I didn't know he meant that night. I also assumed that fish slept when the moon was out. I was even more surprised when Jeff, Spencer's cousin, climbed into the jeep behind me.

Jeff was a couple of years younger and had never been more than fifty miles from the place where he was born. He didn't look anything like his cousin, being only about five feet seven inches tall with sandy blond hair and blue eyes. Jeff always had a warm smile on his face, like a child who had just gotten away with doing something wrong.

Spencer drank a beer as we drove over the rough backroads towards the river, while Jeff cracked jokes. I was relaxed but frustrated as hell. Values are completely different in this wild, wonderful land of West Virginia. Keeping up with the latest trends isn't important. The locals I've met are happy being who they are—they don't need to copy someone else.

At the river, Jeff picked up his fishing gear and walked downstream. Spencer removed the rest of the gear, but made no move toward the water. He put the cooler next to a large rock and sat on the ground, his back against the boulder. After opening a beer for himself, he handed me one. I sat across from him. The moon was bright, and I could see his free hand. It was cupped around the ever present, prominent bulge in his jeans.

Spencer, who was always sure of himself, broke the silence,

startling me. "I figure it's time we had us a talk, Keith. Folks round here might seem strange to an outsider, specially a flatlander like yourself. It doesn't take us long to make up our minds about things. When a young, good-looking man comes into the area and he doesn't have anything to do with the women, then we just figure him to be a queer."

I was caught so completely off guard, I wouldn't have been able to respond even if he had given me the chance.

"Most folks in these parts don't understand queers, but as long as they leave the kids alone, nobody will hassle them. Hell, most people in these hills have something to hide. I myself learned in the Navy that it felt a lot better to let some guy suck on my big old peter than it did to get them damn penicillin shots after fuckin around with some cheap hooker. You've probably heard stories 'bout us country boys fuckin' sheep? Well I only know one guy who's done that. The rest of us, well some of us, just fuck each other when we can't find a girl who's willing. Hell, man, I've been shovin' my cock up Jeff's ass for a long time. The difference is 'round here we don't talk about it. I've fucked some guys who were better than some girls; Jeff is one of them. You've made some of the right moves getting involved in things with the guys. You just need to take out a girl now and then, be seen in public with her, and everyone will leave you alone if that's what you want. I thought bringing you out here tonight would be a good idea. I know you want me. The last couple of times we've been out drinkin' I had to go home and beat my meat because of the way you stared at my crotch all night. If I'm wrong, and you don't want it, just say so and we'll do some fishin'."

I said some pretty dumb things, asking what I had done to give myself away, without really wanting to know, mostly just tripping over my words. It had been months since I had been with a man and now this sexy beast was offering himself to me, no strings attached.

Spencer then stood and walked toward me, "Maybe you want to see what you'd be getting."

He stopped about three feet away and peeled off his red plaid shirt and shucked his jeans. There was more cock hanging between his long legs than I could think of a use for. Suddenly, as if by reflex, I was on my knees. I unzipped my jeans and pulled out my rigid meat. I started pumping on it as Spencer walked closer. He stopped just out of my reach and asked if I wanted to get Jeff in on the action. I nodded. Jeff wasted no time removing his clothes when he saw what was happening. I leaned forward and took Spencer's thriving manhood in my mouth. The days and nights of frustration melted as my tongue explored his mammoth rod. Jeff shoved my hand aside and began to work on my pole. It was better than any dream, and the best was still to come.

Spencer pulled his wonderful cock from my mouth, and Jeff helped me undress. Wanting me to fuck him, he stretched out on the soft pine needles. I fell on top of him and Jeff raised his firm, round ass in search of my cock. I was almost crazed as I drove into him. I continued to shove forward, loving the gentle purring sound he made. I had almost forgotten Spencer as I pounded my desire into Jeff's warm ass.

Spencer walked around and sat down above Jeff's head. He spread his legs, one on each side of his cousin's head. Jeff raised his face, opened his mouth, and sucked on Spencer's balls. I lifted my head and took the huge steel beam of joy into my mouth, while I continued to pile drive into Jeff's receptive hole. Feeling my cum reaching a boiling point and knowing I was about to spill into my victim's ass, I released Spencer's cock and threw my head back. I heard Spencer mutter, "Pound the hell out of that ass! That's the way he likes it."   So did I.

I was totally exhausted and breathless when I rolled off Jeff onto my back. Jeff didn't move. Opening my eyes, I looked up at Spencer. He was slowly working his hand up and down his long, thick pole.

"Well," he sighed, "I don't know which of you to fuck first. But I guess it's been a long time since the flatlander has had any, so I'll plug him first. Don't worry, Jeff, old buddy, I'll get to you."

Spencer told me to follow him. Stopping in front of a tree, he kicked my feet, causing me to spread my legs. He pushed me, telling me to lean forward and put my hands on the tree. Placing one hand on my shoulder, his finger dug into my flesh. I could feel his body against mine, his tool between my legs. I looked down and saw the head of his long, super cock against my balls. Then I felt it being lifted and pushed against my ass. Spencer entered me hard, using just a drop of saliva. Releasing my shoulder, he put his hands on each side of my waist, holding my ass firmly in place. I didn't think he would ever get the whole thing in me, but once he did I was in heaven.

He fucked me with long driving thrusts, pulling his dick almost all the way out then ramming it back in. I was so lost in pleasure, I didn't notice Jeff until he crawled between me and the tree on his knees. He wrapped his lips around my cock. I couldn't have asked for more. I filled Jeff's mouth with my hot juice almost at the same time Spencer's equipment erupted in my ass.

I thought I would fall over when Spencer pulled his piece of meat from my ass. I turned and leaned back against the tree, watching my fucker lie down on his back, his cock still at full mast. Jeff walked over and stood astride of him, before falling to his knees. Jeff then reached around and guided Spencer's fantastic stick between the cheeks of his ass, before sitting down with a quick swift movement. He began to ride Spencer's cock with a sure sense of what he was doing. He had that same childlike smile on his face as he rode the monster. Jeff was stroking his own meat as I stood above them pumping my cock. Spencer arched his back, lifting his ass and his cousin from the ground as he filled Jeff's ass with a hot load. At about the same time, Jeff dumped his juice on Spencer's chest. Just a second later, I felt a churning in my balls and I was shooting my sweet cream into Jeff's golden hair. I watched as the white cream dropped onto Spencer's beautiful face.

The only emotion involved in these acts had been raw, savage lust, but they'd been satisfying beyond description. After this first encounter, I knew a night out with the boys could lead to about anything—and it did. Spencer introduced me to a couple of guys whose wives were in the last months of pregnancy, and I wound up providing a real service. None, however, ever compared with Spencer.

I was best man at Spencer's wedding a year later. The night before the ceremony after a stag party, we went back to the river and he fucked me four times before dawn. After the wedding service in a small country church, Jeff and I were standing side by side watching Spencer and his new wife walk toward their jeep. I wondered what Jeff was thinking. My mind was filled with thoughts of our past good times and a little envy.

Spencer helped his bride into the jeep and then instead of getting in and driving away, he walked over to where Jeff and I were standing. I looked around nervously, but no one seemed to notice. Spencer slapped me on the back and shook hands with Jeff.

"Look buddies, I plan to have one hell of a time this week-end. You two do the same. Get some beer and head back to Rob's cabin. I'll keep score of how any times I get off, and you two keep a tally. We'll get together Monday night, and the winner gets to choose who fucks who."

Jeff and I both laughed as Spencer drove away, and I knew I was going to give Jeff's ass a real workout over the next couple of days. I was going to win the contest and have the first shot of the newlywed's cum up my ass.

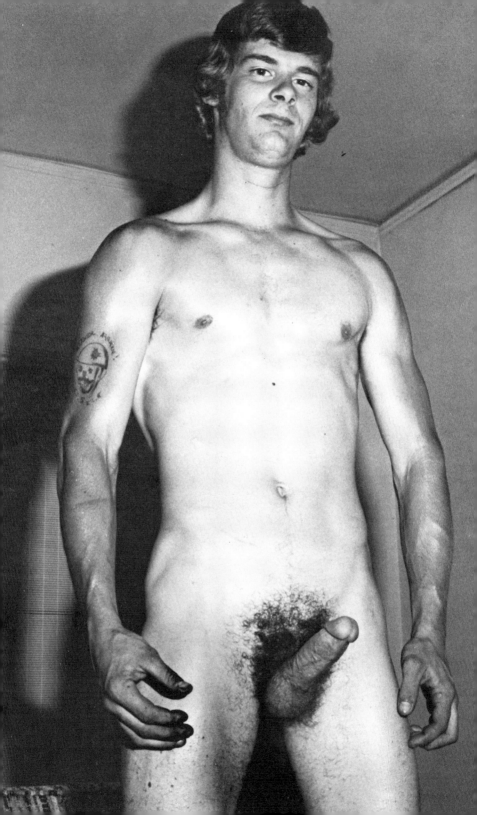

Tommy Has Gorgeous Meat

When I was in college a few years ago, I came to realize my true sexual preference. I had been fascinated by young men's bodies for some time. At school, I had spent as much time as possible around the locker rooms. I used to pretend I was a girl voyeur, secretly savoring the male nudity all around.

When I got an erection, which was often, I carefully hid it.

In college, it came to me that it wasn't the bodies of my peers that excited me—it was the bodies of younger men. That's when I began visiting the locker rooms of YMCA's and the gymnasiums of high schools.

On Saturday afternoons, I would go to a movie—one which seemed to have appeal to the objects of my desire. After my eyes became accustomed to the darkness, I would look for one sitting alone and take the seat beside him. My objective was to feel his cock and try to excite him into an erection. Putting one foot on the opposite knee would project the first knee over his legs. Then I would put my hand under the knee, so my hand lightly touched his pants. If he didn't move away—and he seldom did—I would get bolder and let my whole hand rest on the top of his pants just under the zipper. Now there was no question about what I was after.

I felt for his cock and usually found it hard or getting hard. Now I would play with it using my forefingers and my thumb to ease down his zipper. Reaching in over his jockey shorts, I'd get a good feel of his hard dick. At this point, one of three things would likely happen. He might become alarmed and move away. Or he might move his hand over to my fly to play with my cock, which was, of course, hard as a rock. This would cause me to shoot my wad. When this was about to happen, I would move his hand away, pull out my handkerchief and come in my pants. Then I would leave, quite to the boy's surprise. The third reaction would be a street-wise one. He'd offer to go to the men's room with me if I would give him five bucks. Once there, he would expect me to jack him off. In the case of one handsome conquest, he asked me to blow him, which I did. It was the greatest thrill of my life up to that time.

After law school, I was a struggling young attorney in a Connecticut city. There I became more and more obsessed. Then one day I met Tommy, who lived a couple of houses away. When I was raking my lawn one afternoon, he came by on his bike and stopped to chat. He was friendly and natural, and in ten minutes I knew all about him. He was the second oldest of four—with an older brother and two younger sisters. His father, a CPA, and his mother, a civic activist, were seldom home. Tommy liked soccer and baseball, and when he could find someone to go with, skiing and fishing. I thought he was the most beautiful creature I had ever seen and immediately fell in love.

It was natural that I should become a surrogate father, and as time passed we were together frequently. I kept my sexual desires pretty well under wraps for several months—until his birthday. On that day, he came over to see me—knowing full well I had a present for him. And so I did—a very nice trout fishing rod.

He sat beside me on the couch while he opened it. "It's really cool, John. Will you take me fishing soon?"

"You bet," I said.

"Maybe we can take an overnight fishing trip and sleep together in a cabin or a tent."

"Here, sit between my legs," I said, "and we'll put the rod together."

So I spread my legs, and he sat with his ass right up against my throbbing cock. I reached one hand around him, so it rested squarely on his fly, and lo and behold his rod was hard. He appeared not to notice as I gently unzipped his fly, unbuttoned his pants, reached under his shorts, and began stroking his prick. It was larger than I had visualized, and there was quite a bit of pubic hair. I opened my fly, took out my cock, and pressed it against him. Only then did Tommy stop fiddling with the fishing rod and pay attention to what was happening.

"That feels good," he said as he leaned his head back against my chest, so my nose was in his hair. I drank in the aroma of his hair.

Now nothing could hold me back. I swung him around, so he was lying on his back. I knelt beside the couch and pulled his jeans and shorts down below his knees. That cock was standing straight up—about six inches—just waiting to be serviced. It was a gorgeous circumcised piece of meat, erected above two perfectly proportioned balls. I licked all around—in his virgin pubic hair, under his balls and between his legs, on his balls themselves, and then I started up that magnificent shaft—kissing, licking, and nipping. When I reached the head and put it in my mouth, Tommy put his hands on my head and pressed me down. He moved upward with his hips so that the entire rod was in my mouth. I tasted a drop of pre-cum and then came the ejaculation—there was not great volume, but it was the most marvelous fluid ever to go down my throat. By sheer will power I kept myself from coming, and I kept him in my mouth until he became soft and pulled away.

He got up, pulled up his pants as though nothing had happened, and went to the bathroom. When he came out, he astounded me by saying, "Hey, John, have you ever been corn-holed?"

"God, no! How did you hear about that?"

"Some of the guys used to do it at camp. But I never did. But I think I'd like to do it to you."

I was astonished and at the same time excited. "Listen, Tommy, this is serious business. You think about it, and if tomorrow you still want to, that's O.K. with me."

So my prince left me and I jerked off, just thinking about tomorrow. That night I gave myself an enema and had nothing but liquids for dinner and breakfast. The next morning, I gave myself another enema. Then Tommy arrived. "I've thought about it, John, and I still want to do it. O.K. with you?"

Was it O.K. with me? He got his answer by looking at the bulge in my pants. He got the message and took charge. We went to my bedroom, and he told me to take off my clothes and lie on my stomach. While I watched transfixed, he undressed and displayed the divine, quivering cock. "I read about this in a dirty book," he said, "so I know I should use some Vaseline. Got any?"

I directed him to the medicine cabinet where he found some. He then proceeded to slather his rod. When he came up to the bed, I shuddered in ecstasy as he applied some to my asshole and then more up inside me.

He lay on top of me, I spread my legs apart, and I felt the probing rod start to explore. He guided it into the hole and then began to push. I relaxed as best I could and felt it penetrate my sphincter. At that point, he reached under me and put his hand around my cock. He started to pump, with his hips and his hand. I was about to come, and he seemed to sense it because at the moment of my orgasm, he shot his precious fluid inside me. This was the high point of my affair with Tommy. We remained good friends, and over the next couple of years I blew him a few times, but we never talked about the corn-holing incident. Then he went away to college, and his family moved away. The last I heard, he had gotten a teen-age girl pregnant and had married her.

—*Northford, Connecticut*

105

Circle Jerk

*I*ve only participated in one circle-jerk in all my varied career. It was while I was in high school, in Oregon. There was a Scout camp up in the woods above the lake, and I was up there with four other boys one summer weekend: Jack, Charlie, Harry, and Ron. Charlie was a very hot, hunky guy, and he filled his jeans in a very exciting way. Ron was a cute-looking kid, complete with freckles, dimpled grin, and a painful shyness. Jack was pretty much of a hoodlum, very fond of making manly gestures of strength and daring. Harry was just an average guy, and he took delight in embarrassing Ron, who blushed like a radish at the slightest provocation.

We'd cooked our dinner over a fire and were sitting around bullshitting about various things. Harry got on Ron's case about being so shy, and he said something like: "Jeez, Ronny, you ain't ever gonna get a piece of ass if you don't do something about that. I'll bet if some girl offered herself to you on a silver platter, you'd be so shy about it that you probably couldn't even get your dick up."

Ron turned red. Charlie chimed in: "Shit, Ron, you gotta get used to gettin' close to people. Now, me, if some chick did that . . . offered herself . . . I'd just haul out The Champ and show her what it's for."

Ron turned redder. The razzing continued, and Ron finally got angry at being teased, and said: "Hey, will you guys talk about something else?"

Harry wouldn't let up. "No kiddin', Ron . . . you should take lessons from Charlie! . . . even Jack, for that matter, although he ain't got much to show anybody."

Jack responded with a "Go fuck yourself, asshole! I got just as much as anybody here!" That led to a challenge from Harry for everybody to "take it out and we'll see who's got the biggest one." He had his own out in a couple of seconds. It was soft, uncut, and appeared to be a bit larger than the average.

Charlie chuckled: "Christ, that's nothing!" . . . and he proceeded to bring forth a cock nearly twice the size of Harry's. It was also soft, cut, and it swayed magnetically.

As far as I knew, I was the only guy there who was a confirmed homosexual. I'd already had a couple of romps with Jack and one with Ron. I knew that Jack had a little over six inches, and that Ron's cock was really big, about eight or maybe more. I was so excited by what was going on that I had a hard-on, and I was a bit shy, myself, about taking it out. When I had it fully exposed, both Charlie and Harry made wisecracks about me being horny. I said: "Well, we can't say who's the biggest unless they're all hard, can we?" Jack hauled his out, and it was hard, too. Ron blinked as he looked around, and he looked absolutely mortified. We all began taunting him to show us his cock, but he just couldn't bring himself to do it. Jack led the pack: "Let's pants him!"

Poor Ron was helpless, and though he struggled, we soon had him flat on the ground. His pants were pulled down, exposing his bulging Jockeys. Charlie deftly grabbed the waistband of those shorts and slid them to Ron's ankles, and his beautiful hard cock was there for all to see. The one time I'd seen it before was during a ride in my Model A. I stopped in a secluded place I liked to use for such events, and proceeded to seduce him into letting me play with his cock. It took a lot of work, since he was so reticent and embarrassed . . . but I finally managed to grope him, and was astonished at the size of what I felt. At last, he let me take it out. When I took hold of it and stroked it, he grabbed his legs and gasped. It took him only thirty or forty seconds to shoot his load . . . all over his clothes and my hand. When he was through coming, I sat back and jacked off, and he watched me with wide eyes.

Now that we had Ron exposed, Charlie was less proud of his own equipment. He played with himself and got a hard-on, and those two cocks, Ron's and Charlie's, proved to be almost the same in length and thickness. The only difference was that Ron's was heavily veined, while Charlie's was smooth as a bar of hardwood.

It was Jack who suggested the circle-jerk. "Let's see who can shoot the farthest." He described a line with the heel of his boot, and everybody got up to it, even Ron, and all five cocks were being stroked furiously. I noted, by the way, that Charlie kept his eyes fixed on Ron, who was standing next to him. Harry had his eyes closed, and Jack was staring straight ahead, like someone in a trance. I, on the other hand, was checking out the entire ensemble. Ron came first, and he shot a few feet. Harry and Charlie were a dead heat for the second place, with Harry firing his cum a good five feet. I followed Harry, and my cum landed near Ron's. Jack took a long time to shoot, and we all watched him and encouraged him, and the veins and cords of his neck were standing in relief. When he shot, it came in extremely rapid squirts, two or more per second, and his went about as far as Ron's and mine. Harry was the proud victor.

"I really think this is saving our marriage, Edgar."

It wasn't until two summers later that I got to suck Ron's cock. We were working on the sets for a show at school, and I managed to seduce him in the prop room backstage. I steered the conversation to sex, and it had just the right effect on him; Ron quickly showed a fine bulge in his pants. When I was sure that he was hot enough to try anything, I asked him if he'd like me to suck him off. He blinked his eyes, gulped, and nodded his head slowly. That was one of the finest blowjobs I can remember giving anybody. He sat on a tall stool, with his fine cock and balls presented for my delectation, and I just plain feasted on him. The more I licked and mouthed his balls, the more he squirmed and writhed . . . and when I tongued my way up to the head of his cock, he was quickly heading for the homestretch.

In case I haven't made it clear by now, I'm a lifelong cock worshipper. That's no exaggeration, by the way. I paid reverent homage to Ron's cock and balls with my hands and mouth, and was thrilled by his responses. When he was about to let go, he whispered, "If you don't want it in your mouth, you better stop now!"

Well, I sure as hell wanted it! With two handfuls of my hair held tightly, Ron gave me his load of cum. The shyness was all gone, and he was reveling in the glorious feeling of coming in a friend's mouth., His cum was very salty and rather bitter, but I savored it. I can taste it even now!

—*San Francisco, California*

The Man With Big Thighs

My first homosexual experience occurred when I was young, and it was absolutely incredible. At the time, my mother and father were divorced, and I hadn't seen my father in years. Even then, I was sexually very mature and horny. A friend of mine and I used to look at his father's nude girlie magazines furtively and jerk off together, and I jerked off by myself every time I got a chance. I was so preoccupied with sex and jerking off that I couldn't concentrate on school and homework, so my grades were terrible. As a result, my mother hired a man that lived in our apartment building to give me private tutoring. My mother worked a late shift in the afternoon and evening, so the man (his name was Brian) and I spent our sessions alone in my apartment.

Brian was a really nice guy. He was about forty years old, tall and nice looking. I remember the first time I met him I noticed he had exceptionally large thighs and a big ass which really stretched his pants tight, although from the waist up he wasn't particularly big. Whenever he would come over to tutor me, he would sit beside me on the sofa and sooner or later, he would be so close that one of his big thighs would be resting firmly against mine. At first, I would try to move away a little, but it always seemed that he would just move again so that his thigh would soon be back against mine. After a few sessions like this, I noticed that his thigh felt really good against mine, and I quit trying to move away. Once that happened, it seemed like he got a lot more familiar with me physically. He would put his hand on my leg continually or else put his hand on my shoulder. As the physical contact continued, I began to think that maybe Brian was "queer" which produced a real conflict in me. On the one hand, I felt it was somehow wrong to sit so close to a man with him putting his hands all over me so frequently. On the other hand, I had to admit that I really enjoyed it, and at that point, he had not done anything which could be considered to be definitely out of line.

Later, I realized that Brian was a master at seduction. He really knew how to take his time and not scare me off. The first time he really stepped up the action occurred about two months after he had started tutoring me. We were sitting together on the couch with his leg pressed up tight against mine as usual. It was about five o'clock in the afternoon, and my mom had left for work about an hour before. I answered some homework questions for Brian, and to my surprise, he said, "Jerry, I'm so proud of the progress you've made that I just have to give you a kiss."

Before I could react or say anything, he moved his head down and pressed his full smooth lips to mine. The feeling of his mouth on mine made my head swim with excitement, and I felt my cock starting to harden quickly. Still, he was playing it slow and cool, and he broke the kiss after a few seconds and acted as if he had just been expressing his affection for me for being a good student. I was a little confused, but my confusion cleared up when the tutoring session ended a little later, and Brian said, "How about a goodbye kiss?"

Again, before I could say anything, he pressed his lips against mine, only this time he left them there a little longer. Just as before, my head began to swim and my cock began to get hard, particularly when he pushed his tongue into my mouth, and at the same time began to feel up my legs.

After about a minute of this, my cock was harder and more erect than it had ever been in my life, even though he still had not touched it or done anything more than feel my thighs. He finally broke the kiss, and smiling at me, he said, "Do you like to kiss like this, Jerry?"

All I could do was murmur, "Oh, yes, Brian, it feels so good."

He moved his mouth back to mine and began kissing me passionately, at the same time moving his hand to my cock and massaging it through my pants. In a few seconds, I felt the cum rising in me, and I knew I was going to shoot off any minute. I broke the kiss and said, "Jesus, I'm about to cum."

He smiled and said, "Take it out quick."

I quickly unzipped my Levi's and pulled my jockey shorts down over my rock-hard cock. Just as it began to jerk, he lowered his mouth to it and fastened his lips around my swollen dickhead. I just exploded at that moment, and I could feel my dick jerking so hard that it actually hurt as I shot squirt after squirt of cum into his sucking mouth. I had never felt anything so wonderful in my life. I was still hard after I finished pumping. When he finally had all of my load in his mouth, he stopped sucking and said, "Why don't we go over to my fuckin' apartment? We can get nude there and really have some sexy fuckin' fun." Hearing him talk dirty was thrilling to me, and put me in a deliciously filthy mood.

Needless to say, he didn't have to ask me twice. I had never before had so much "fuckin" fun, and I was eager for more. When we got to his apartment, we quickly stripped naked, and

I was all eyes as I looked at his nude body. His cock looked enormous to me. It was completely erect, pointing straight up in the air, tight against his belly. It was really wide and fat along the shaft, and the head of it was really big and mushroom-shaped. It was so swollen that it was shiny and purplish in color. I loved it, just as I loved his enormous hairy legs and his big firm ass.

We sat on his sofa for a while and I felt his cock and thighs eagerly. Then he urged me to take his cock in my mouth. I really had to open wide to get that big cockhead in, but once it was in, I found that I just loved its taste and the sexy smell that emanated from around his big balls. I could feel it jerk slightly once in a while, which would then be accompanied by a luscious slightly salty taste in my mouth. I gobbled on the big monster like there was no tomorrow and swallowed his big load eagerly.

Soon, he suggested that we go into his bedroom. His walls were covered with male pinups featuring big powerful body-builders, all of them with big erect cocks, and many of them decked out in leather garments such as black leather hoods, masks, boots, thigh belts, wrist bands, and other exciting outfits. I was so sexed up that I couldn't believe it. By the time I left that evening, he had taught me the fun of heavy male necking, body worship, ball sucking, 69, and, best of all, rimming.

Over the next four years, Brian and I did every hot fucking sex act that two horny males can do together, including fist fucking after my rectum had opened up sufficiently. I loved getting my face between his big ass cheeks and sucking his asshole. I also loved sucking his balls, cock, tits, and licking and worshipping his huge hairy legs. Even to this day, nothing turns me on like a pair of extra big, hairy thighs and calves. Brian also turned me on to sadistic fantasy, and we popped many a load together imagining we were dungeon masters, listening to discipline tapes with headphones. I would love even now to get into some heavy S&M action with some big-legged, fucking leatherman, but for many reasons, I have to confine my current homosexual activity to an occasional session in a hotel room or else a good hot telephone scene with some other big stud. Your magazine is really good, so how about a feature on big leg worship? All of us big leg lovers would appreciate it!

—*Marina Del Rey, California*

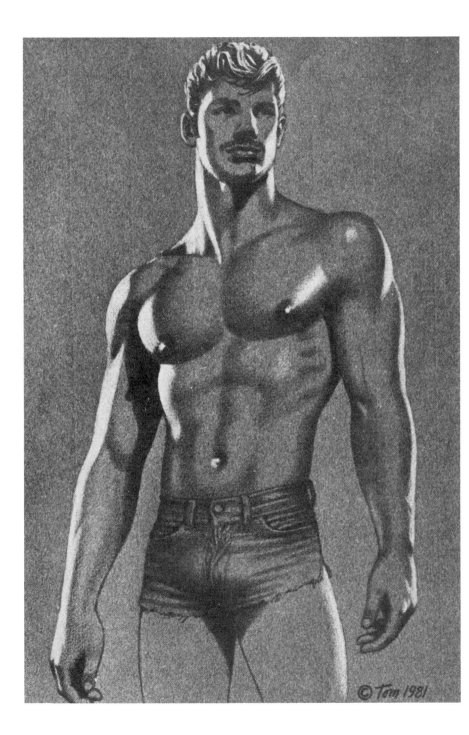
© Tom 1981

Herring Cove

B Y   R I C K   C H A N D L E R

*T*he July sun beat down furiously on Provincetown's Herring Cove beach. I had walked a long distance from the parking lot, thrown down a large beach towel, squeezed half a tube of *Bain de Soleil* over me and lay back, overwhelmed with thought.

I proudly smiled at the successful lies and excuses that got me my ticket aboard the Greyhound bus. I had arrived at Commercial Street only hours ago, and at sixteen, this was my first experience away from home without my parents hovering nearby. What my folks thought I was doing and the truth of the matter were worlds apart, and they'd remain that way for the next two weeks.

The purpose of this trip was sex—something I had never had, that's if you don't count masturbating at muscle magazines stolen from newsstands. I knew I had to find out what my powerful urges toward men were about.

Having heard of this summer resort for homosexuals, I had become obsessed with this visit. Well, there I was, having played all my cards, alone, with no idea what to do, surrounded by the men I hoped would deal me in for whatever the game was. I wanted it and I was terribly afraid of it. Since I didn't know how to make a move, I was counting on my age, my blond, waspish good looks, and my body which was sensually somewhere between lithe adolescence and sexy maturity.

A gust of wind-blown sand interrupted my thoughts. I sat up, realizing that the images of sex were stretching the thin material of my bathing suit. I looked around and saw men, all older than me, playing at the game of being gay. Of all the beaches I could have selected, I had somehow zeroed in on this gay one like a homing pigeon. But that was easy. There'd been practically a parade of men marching straight to this beach from the guest house I had registered into.

Now I was intimidated and overwhelmed. Turning on my stomach, I pretended to read *Sons and Lovers,* required summer reading for my junior year in high school. Soon, however, my eyes were drifting up to the dunes bordering the beach. Along the ridge, an occasional singular man stood and watched, while others filed silently by, some disappearing over the top to the other side. My youthful ignorance prevented me from perceiving what was going on, but I was aware that there was something intense and forbidden that I had to see.

As I sheepishly walked toward the first set of dunes, too nervous to look up, I watched my feet molest the sand. I even thought of when I used to dig holes on the beach not so many years ago. This was a vastly different world, and the thought momentarily chilled me.

Mounting the ridge, I was astounded at the panorama. An endless cloud of white sand confronted me, long flat stretches broken only by tall mounds. In the distance I could see men rambling about, while others remained still on the peaks of various dunes. It was as if each had won at playing *King of the Hill.* Yet this was a different game entirely, a quite serious one.

Continuing across a stretch of flat, packed sand, I felt the intensity of watchful eyes on me. Finally I trudged up a steep incline of an unguarded dune. It was empty except for clumps of bright green beach grass that whistled in the breeze.

Nearing the top, I was breathless after so much walking and from nervous anticipation. I wanted to reach my goal and rest. I needed a break, time to rest and figure out what to do next, even if that was to just stand there like everyone else.

When I reached the wide, flat top, I was shocked to find a man lying naked on a blanket. He appeared to be asleep. Deeply tanned and muscular, he shimmered from suntan oil and sweat that reflected the sun. He lay on his back, with his brown hair wet and tousled and his handsome head tossed back like a wild stallion's. His neck was supported by a rolled-up pair of faded jeans. I was stunned.

Letting my eyes travel further down from his face, I gazed at his solid, muscular chest that was topped with curls of brown hair funneling down to a navel, centered on a hard, flat stomach. Below that, a greased cock lay across his hip like a fat, fleshy snake. Its size and weight made it droop over his hip, allowing me to see the outline of its head under the foreskin that shielded it from the sun. I remember thinking that that was the only part of his body even remotely hidden from view. His legs were spread slightly, and a large sac, stretched from the heat, carried two huge balls that rested on the blanket.

He was such a picture of raw, male sex that I was staring for probably several minutes before realizing that he was more than an apparition. This was no desert mirage. A real, hot-blooded man was stretched out in front of me. Embarrassed at myself, I turned to leave him, thinking that I had broken the rules. This was *his* dune and I had trespassed.

"Now that you've looked, couldn't you at least say 'hello'?"

He wasn't asleep after all. Had he seen me standing there foolishly all this time?

"I didn't mean to wake you," was all I could muster in response.

"You didn't. I was waiting until you'd finished surveying the territory. Make up your mind?"

"About what?"

"You know very well. About me."

I was trapped. Was this a proposition?

"I couldn't help but notice you." Another stupid comment.

"I'm sure you couldn't, since I'm the only one here."

The handsome stranger began massaging his cock which was now as wide awake as he was. Each time he pulled on it, the foreskin would slide back, offering a glimpse of the large, white head underneath—the only part of him that wasn't bronzed by the sun. I had a fascination about seeing this one, hidden part of him.

"My name's Bill. Do you want to come over and get your feet off the hot sand?"

"Sure," I said, trying to sound confident.

As I walked the few feet to his blanket, he moved over to make room for me, while brazenly looking me up and down. He flashed a seductive smile.

"You're awfully young, aren't you."

"Eighteen," I lied.

"Good. I like young guys like you. Makes me feel a hell of a lot older, though. I'm twenty-nine."

So is my uncle, my mother's youngest brother, I thought. I sat on the blanket. Bill laughed, probably at my shy awkwardness, and leaned back, again stroking his enormous prick. It was now stiff and erect.

"You like that, huh?" he said as he made a point of looking at his cock and displaying it with his hand. "Ten inches hasn't hurt my dating record," he announced proudly.

I was paralyzed with desire and apprehension, wondering what to do.

"Are you new at this?" he said.

"I haven't had much experience." I'd had none.

"All the better," he said. "I teach high school all year, and I don't mind teaching you a few things even though I'm on vacation."

There was no turning back, and I knew it. He put his large, masculine hand on my thigh and stroked it, soon moving onto the fabric against my leg, teasing my already hard cock. Then he slid around on the blanket, turning me with him, so that he was lying next to me. Stretching one leg over me, he turned me onto my back and sat up, straddling my thighs. He was strong and in control. Tugging at my Speedo swimsuit, he yanked it down to my knees, then off my legs.

Naked and trapped underneath him, I looked up at his chest which blocked the sun. He leaned over and took my cock in his hand, stroking it. This was the first time a man had touched it. Suddenly he leaned over and took my cock in his mouth. I gasped and felt a surge of excitement as he circled the head with his soft, expert tongue. It felt as if all the energy in my body was focused on my cock and that his mouth was in complete command. I was vaguely aware of gulls crying in the background, but except for that there was nothing else in the world as far as I was concerned.

While he sucked and licked enthusiastically, one hand moved around to squeeze my ass. I was so excited by his tongue that I barely noticed when his fingers began to probe at my asshole. Then one slipped inside and I flinched. This was something I never dreamed of. When I thought of sex I had only thought of cocks. Without a word, he removed his finger and slowly sat upright. As he was still straddling me, he inched his way up and over my chest until his enormous rod and huge hanging balls were only inches from my face. I saw the thick veins stretching up the sides of his massive warhead, pumping the blood that made it so hard. My heart beat faster and faster as he took it in his hand and teased my lips with its head, brushing it back and forth across my mouth. Finally, he held it still in front of my mouth and pushed it gently between my lips.

I tasted the head which was glistening already with drops of cum. He pushed further, I gagged once, then began to savor this morsel. I licked it like a deprived child who had finally been given a piece of candy. Soon I had taken practically the whole length in my throat.

He moved it in and out and began to fuck my face, his balls slapping against my chin with every forward thrust. Then he slipped it out and arched higher so that his smooth sac was lying on my mouth. It was warm and greased like the rest of his body. Instinctively, I began to take one, then both balls into my mouth. He moaned and told me to lick them everywhere, to take them deeper. I was crazed with excitement. My hesitations and fears had dissolved as I wallowed in this freedom, the ecstasy of this first encounter.

Suddenly he pried himself loose from my hungry mouth and with one agile movement was off of me, commanding me to turn over. I did, now lost in the grip of his desires. He was over me again, spreading my legs apart and pushing his head up to my ass until his tongue found its mark. This time I didn't resist. I automatically lifted my pelvis to encourage this new act. Then he stopped and sat up.

Nothing happened for a few moments. I strained my neck to look around, only to see Bill holding a bottle of suntan oil upside down while he squeezed it, letting the liquid, hot from the sun, drip onto my ass and between my legs. Then he squirted more onto his hand, tossed the bottle aside and began massaging his massive cock.

"I'm going to fuck you now," he said matter-of-factly, as if there were no choice. There wasn't. I was scared and tried to twist my body free, but he pinned me down with his strong hands.

"With an ass like that, you're not getting away yet," he said authoritatively.

He grabbed his cock and guided it between my legs as he lay the full length of his body on me. He pushed slowly until I felt his fat, hungry cockhead against my asshole. Suddenly, he thrust harder, entering me slightly, enough to cause me almost to scream in pain. He held firmly and waited until he could sense me relax. Then he pushed further and further until all ten inches had found their way in. After lingering for several seconds, he began pulling it out and pushing it back. It hurt and then it didn't. I began to relax more and even followed his rhythm with my hips. He moved faster and faster until he was moaning and breathing heavily in my ear. The sweat between us was mixing and making our skin slide against each other.

Soon, I was totally abandoned to this man's incredible cock pounding faster and harder with every thrust. My own cock was stiff with excitement as it rubbed back and forth on the blanket. Soon he groaned louder and said, simply, "I'm coming." Then with a final push, hot spurts of cum were shooting inside of me. Just as suddenly, I felt a shudder and I shot a load of thick cum onto the blanket and my stomach. It seemed to never end. With a long sigh, Bill collapsed on me, panting heavily.

When he was able to catch his breath, he said, "Either I'm a good teacher, or you're a good student."

I've changed teachers since, but I haven't changed majors. And I'm studying harder than ever.

Army Lieutenant Likes Gay Nookie

I am a twenty-four-year-old reader of your magazine, who really enjoys the reader stories. Presently, I am a lieutenant in the Army, stationed in Louisiana.

My story is how I got into sex with other guys. I was young the first time.

My parents were well off, and we lived in a large house in California. One afternoon, I think it was late summer, I was swimming in our pool and the gardener, Eddie, walked over. He started talking about his latest girl friend and the "piece" he scored the night before. Eager to hear more I pressed close to the side of the pool. He sat down, took off his old Army boots, and began wading in the water.

I questioned him extensively on the girls he'd had. Eddie was a real bullshitter, but at the time I took it as sacred. As our conversation progressed, he began relating to me how good it felt to have a girl go down on you. I was quite naïve, so curiosity took hold of me when he offered to show me how it was done.

We moved into the cabana, and he had me wait while he got his girlie books from his cottage. My mother really over-protected me then, and I had never seen or heard of such books. Entranced, I stared as he turned the pages, exposing my eyes to those buxom beauties. I was quickly caught up in the excitement of this forbidden pleasure.

Eddie turned to the second book, and when I opened to the centerfold, I saw a man with a huge penis being sucked off by a very young girl. I marveled at the picture and asked Eddie if all men's things were that big. He got to laughing so hard, it almost hurt my feelings. Then in a moment of tenderness, he pulled me close. "Say kid, don't worry! Ole Eddie here taught all his brothers and most of his cousins about the facts of life, so I'll tell you, too."

Listening intently to his every word, I soon discovered all about sex and babies and whores and nice girls. Then he began explaining about masturbation. I had been rubbing off for some time already and knew it felt good. He then suggested that I should let him look at my penis, so he could tell me how I compared with other boys my age.

Sheepishly I stood up, peeling off my swim trunks. Standing only in my wet underpants, he approached me. We were both giggling, and he seemed as nervous as I was. Opening the elastic waistband and peering in at my meat, he announced I might be old enough to cum. He then sank down on his knees and removed my underpants. Standing in the cabana with this twenty-two-year-old gardener, all naked and everything, I felt goosepimples all over my skin. Slowly he began pumping the little hard-on I had developed. Using saliva, he went down the head and began a faster rhythm. My legs were unsteady, and I felt as if I was going to pass out. "Hey, you're a live one, aren't you?"

He asked if I was ready for more. Unknowingly, I nodded yes. He took his tongue and began licking the head of my pee-pee. I trembled and fell back. Reassuringly, he caught me and helped me to the towel on the floor. Eddie smiled at me and asked if I liked that. Oh, I did indeed! He dove down between my legs, hungrily licking my groin. It was so intense, I closed my eyes and covered them with my hands. His warm tongue soon probed its way around my testicles. It kinda tickled, and I began thrashing about. My body, alive and vibrating, seemed to excite him to no end. He mumbled how good I tasted as he lowered his mouth onto my pouncing erection. This time he took it all, wrapping his talented tongue around it, then pulling it up and down.

He was playing with his erection through his uniform. At my suggestion, he pulled his pants down and proudly displayed his manhood. My hand drifted towards his red throbbing penis, almost involuntarily. I was torn apart inside. I wanted desperately to touch and taste his cock, just like he had done to me. On the other hand, I had never done or ever seen someone do what we were doing. Throwing my fears aside, I took his penis partly in my mouth (it was a decent 7 inches). I was pretty clumsy and, after a few critiques from Eddie, I managed to hold up my end of our little "69."

He was masturbating as I kissed and sucked the top part of his erection. After a few seconds, he was shooting off in my mouth. Scared I pulled back as cum spurted on my face and chest. He continued on hastily sucking mine until I had a dry orgasm. He swore he tasted a little but not very much. I was excited, and Eddie and me grew real close. He, thereafter, would take me anywhere my ma would allow. Somehow he smuggled me into a dirty movie one night. While I sat in the chair, he got his hands down my britches and masturbated me and himself during the good parts of the show. We stopped in the woods on the way back to the house. It was a calm warm

September night. He spread an old blanket on the ground well away from the road. Sensuously, he removed each article of my clothing, tasting and nibbling every inch of my body. I lay back watching him in the moonlight as he also removed all his clothing. He seemed so virile, and I respected him deeply. I guess it was close to a crush.

Our lips met for the first time as he swept me into his strong arms. He had a scent to his person that to this day gives me a hard-on thinking about it. His tongue snaked its way in my mouth, causing me to feel flushed. Instinctively I returned with my tongue. I was totally (physically, mentally, and spiritually) turned on, while his hands kneaded my soft flesh. At the same time, I explored his hairy chest and vey erect penis. He blew on my stomach and on my erection. Licking my legs, thighs, and then turning me over, he forced my cheeks apart. He probed the depths of my anus with his tongue, keeping me aroused for quite a while.

It felt so good and seemed so wrong. I knew from Eddie that guys cool off by pokin' each other in the butt, but I was very unsure I could do it at all. He ate out my hole for at least a half hour. It was a real turn on for me. When he finally ate around to my nuts and penis, I was having another dry orgasm. I mean three licks and I popped. Eddie then pushed his hard-on into my mouth, and I began licking it. He told me to keep swallowing my saliva, and he steadily put his cock in deeper. He got about half of it in before I gagged.

Eddie then withdrew it and hugged me, kissing me into my second hard-on. Reaching into the sack he had brought from the car, he removed some type of lotion. Pushing me on my back and throwing my legs over my shoulders, he applied it to my hole. I was jumping as he pushed his finger in my ass. My eyes felt as if they were gonna bulge out. My mouth was wide open, sucking for air. Oh, how my hole burned something fierce. He pushed his erection around my opening, guiding it with the finger he had buried up me. Then reassuring me that he cared for me, he gently worked the head of his dick up me. Thankfully, the first time he went slow. It did hurt, but it felt so good. Eddie soon shot his creamy load in me, and I knew this is what I wanted.

From then on we grew closer and closer. Eddie was always very attentive to my needs, giving me little gifts like *Playboys*. He even smoked my first joint with me. Once he bought a butt plug and took me to his cottage. After a vigorous blow job session, he lubed the plug and slipped it into my tight hole.

I was surprised to say the least. Eddie told me not to remove it till lunch the following day. Then he would pull it out and reward me. All that night I kept a hard-on. At the dinner table, Dad asked why I was squirming so. At bed time, I skipped my bath and lay flat on my back in bed as Mom tucked me in. She brought her hand across my crotch as she was leaving and noticed my hard-on. She softly murmured as she kissed my forehead that I was becoming quite a man. I loved it. I mean, through Eddie I learned everything about life and love and relationships. Now it seemed that I was growing up at last.

That afternoon I swished as fast as I could to Eddie's cottage. I had to wait till he took his hour break. Finally he showed up and took me into the cottage bedroom. He ordered me to drop my pants and bend over. I quickly complied. He pulled the plug out in one motion, and I fell to the bed in a rush of warmth. With my pants around my ankles, he firmly spread my cheeks and pushed a greased finger up me. Then stripping he started describing what he was gonna do. "You know I'm hot for your ass. How would you like some meat up ya?"

I was really getting scared. He had never talked like this before. It turned me on though, so I guess I liked it. He then greased me up again and in three quick strokes went up and in me. I was startled and in convulsions. My dink flew super hard and this man's man gave me my first and best complete fucking. He pushed his monster up me and I didn't even hardly feel it. My ass had been stretched from that plug, and I had been pushing it deeper all night. Eddie was a real stud. That afternoon he poked me for over forty-five minutes then came in huge spurts. I have been told you can't feel a guy cumming in you, but if so, it did not apply to Eddie. Shees, he poured cum like a fire hydrant.

Shortly, we got into recruiting some of my buddies and having strip poker games that ended up in orgies. Then a few years later, at my friend Mark's birthday, we had all the regular boys over and got drunk. Within twenty minutes we were all naked; there were eight guys and Eddie. We were licking and sucking our brains out. Then we gave Mark his choice of who he wanted to poke for a birthday present. He chose me. We lay down and, while everyone watched, he buried his seven inches in my ass. I looked around, and Scott came over and ran his dick betwen my lips. I sucked it in and deep-throated him.

I was being butt-fucked while slurping another dick, when my Mom looked through the window. She barged into the cottage much to my embarrassment. It wasn't funny then, but when I think back about all of us naked running around a one-room shack, grasping desperately for clothing, it was funny.

The consequences were less so. Eddie packed and ran as fast as he could. The sheriff arrived in twenty minutes at the cottage and found nine or ten angry relatives with guns. With Eddie long gone, the angry parents turned on us. We all got grounded and my folks packed me off to military school. They told me they wantd me to be a man and all that shit.

Sending a homosexual teenager to any kind of boarding school is a very ironic thing. I mean I had so many affairs with upper and lower classmates it was ridiculous. The first week I was there, my roommate and I were already trading licks, and by the second week, a senior cadet was balling me in the shower. During Hell Week, I sucked off or got banged by at least ten different upper classmen. I'd go home in the summer to visit, and that was the only time I'd abstain from my healthy sex life.

When I graduated, I went on to military college and found a regular lover. John was his name, and we fucked for over two years. I have since given blow jobs and been ass-fucked by people in authority in order to get myself promoted. I now have a private lake house where I take recruits for a lick-and-suck session or two. I've never married, because I love my life just the way it is. I did fall for a lady two years ago, but I wasn't happy with our sex life and wound up balling her nineteen-year-old stepbrother; you can say we blew off our relationship.

—*Livingston, Louisiana*

122

"Up Sprang a Very Firm Six Incher"

I was born and raised in a small Southern California beach town. I didn't discover jacking off to orgasm until I was fourteen. Occasionally, I played with myself in bed or while taking a bath. It felt nice, but I just never continued it far enough to get the feeling that something was about to happen.

Like a lot of young teens, I was often cursed with erections at very embarrassing times, such as when riding the school bus, in a classroom, or while walking in the school hall. It was flustering as hell and hard to hide, unless I could cover it with my books or a sweater.

Because of this, I got in the habit of wearing a jockstrap—a very tight one. The smallest I could find was the one made for little guys in the Little League. This worked well. Sometimes I wore it under my jockey shorts, and sometimes I just wore the jockstrap with no other underwear.

One night, while undressing for bed, after I took my tight jock off, I felt itchy in the cock-and-balls area. I presumed the sensation was a result of my wearing the tight jockstrap all day. For relief, I got into bed and started stretching and rubbing myself "down there." I did not get an erection, but I did have a "semi." In fact, without touching my cock, just scratching and massaging, I must have touched a nerve or something. I shot off.

I don't need to tell you how mind-blowingly wonderful it felt. But because I didn't know what it was, it scared the hell out of me. I turned on the light, threw back the covers, and saw all this white slimy stuff. At first, I thought, "Well, thank God it's not blood!" Still, it worried me.

I was tempted to tell my mom. (I lived with Mom, an older brother, and an older sister. My dad had died when I was two.) I decided not to, but instead the next day I told my best buddy, Dick. He was sixteen years old to my fourteen.

Dick said, "Whitey (my nickname, as my hair was so blond it was nearly white), I can't talk now, but I will tell you that it's nothing to worry about. Come on over to my house tonight, and I'll explain it to you."

Well, his folks had left that morning for the weekend, and I could hardly wait until school was out so I could go to Dick's. When I arrived, he asked me to again tell him exactly what happened. I did. Then he proceeded in a very nice way to explain that the stuff that came out of me is called sperm. "It is what makes babies. When a guy has sex with a girl, he should put a rubber on to prevent the sperm from getting in her."

Well, even that was a little over my head. I vaguely knew about rubbers, in that I had seen them on the ground or floating in the water. They were always unrolled. I had never seen a new one and I used to wonder how they were put on. I thought they came unrolled, and that they were just pulled on like gloves. Anyway, I didn't pay much attention to the "rubber" bit. Dick went on to explain that boys get rid of all the excess sperm through wet dreams — which he had to explain — and by masturbation.

When I asked him what masturbation meant, he explained that it meant to jack off. "You do know about jacking off, don't you?" he asked.

Well, I really didn't. I hadn't heard any of my buddies discuss it, so I only vaguely knew what he was touching on. Learning this, Dick decided to not only explain, but to give me a demonstration.

We went into his bedroom. He undressed, propped up the pillows on his bed, and proceeded to show me. He had gotten a towel and a jar of Vaseline. Placing the towel beside him, he proceeded to grease up his cock, explaining as he did that I'd probably find it felt better with lubrication. Dick also recommended butter, mayonnaise, skin lotion, and baby oil.

Soon he was rock hard. Even though he was obviously enjoying himself immensely, Dick instructed as he went along that it felt good to play with your nipples, and fondle your balls with your free hand while jacking off. He showed me how you can grip your cock tightly or loosely and take short fast strokes or long slow sensuous ones. He even showed me that when you are about to reach an orgasm, you should take your hand away and let your cock cool off. Then you can build up the feeling again.

After about twenty minutes of this, he decided he wanted to come, so he told me, "Okay, Whitey, I want to shoot now, so watch carefully." Most of the while, he had been taking long slow strokes. Now he speeded up, then suddenly started taking very slow strokes. With his cock pointed up towards his navel, his cum started spurting forth. It was really a beautiful demonstration.

When he recovered his composure and was cleaning his load off with a towel, he said, "Well, now you know about jacking off.

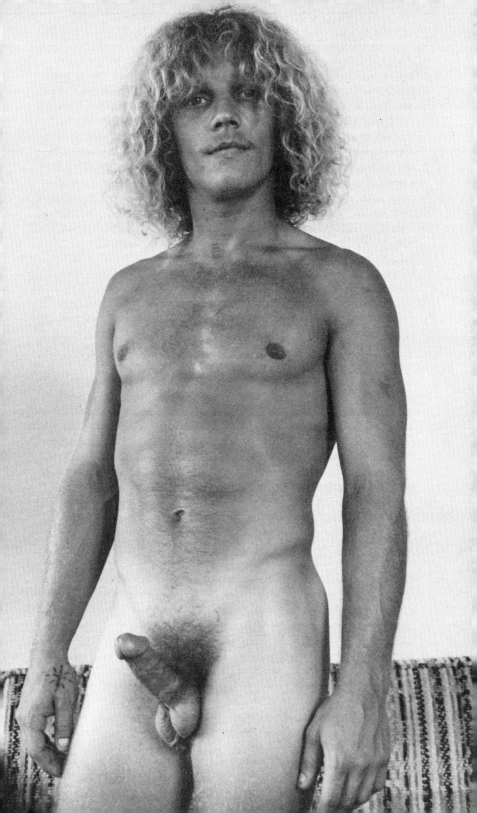

Enjoy yourself, and don't worry about it being bad for you, or that you're doing it too much. You'll know you're doing it too much when your cock refuses to get hard." Soon after that, I had to get home, and Dick had to get ready for a date.

Needless to say, I could hardly wait to try it. Practically running home, I prayed all the while that my mom wouldn't be in. She wasn't, so I ran to the bathroom, took of my T-shirt, lowered my Levi's and pulled down my jockstrap. Up sprang a very firm six-incher. I poured some baby oil in my hand and proceeded. God, it was great! I tried holding back by occasionally taking my hand away, but I was too hot and eager to shoot my first jack-off load. After only two minutes, I really came. My whole body spasmed with orgasm. I immediately cleaned up the mess and was hooked from then on. Three, four, five jerk-offs a day became commonplace.

Very soon after that, I had another mind-blowing experience that not only hooked me, but gave me a strong rubber fetish that is stil with me today.

Our house was on the oceanfront. Oceanfront property is very expensive. As as result, houses are very close together. In some cases, they actually touch. Our neighbor's house was separated from ours by only two and a half feet. A walkway ran between the two houses, from the boardwalk in front to the alley in back. Each end, front and back, had big, solid wooden eight-foot-high gates that we kept locked from the middle so no one could trespass. The neighbors—a mother, father and their seventeen-year-old son—were good friends with my family.

One weekend, Baron, the son, his parents, my family and I were all going to take a trip to Lake Tahoe together. The morning of the day we were to leave, I was out in the ocean body surfing, when Baron came out and joined me. He was really a humpy, cute little guy, about 5' 9" short, with a blonde crewcut, and blue eyes with long thick eyelashes. As he was very athletic—swimming, diving, tennis, etc.—he had a terrific body with wide shoulders, beautiful pecs and lats, a washboard stomach, small waist, cute little spankable buns, and gorgeous, muscular legs. In short, he was a "masturbatory image."

Anyway, as we were swimming and body surfing, he asked me if I was going to Tahoe. At the time I thought I was, so I told him, "Yes." He said, "Well, I'm not. I've been there before. Besides, I've got a hot date tonight." Well, that was that. We soon left the water and went our separate ways.

Much later, as the group was about to leave, I decided I'd rather stay home. My mom agreed, so I was left behind.

I should remind you that our two houses were very close together. Also, Baron's bedroom window was exactly opposite mine. His bed, a captain's bed, sat high since it had pull-out drawers built under it. It was right against the window sill with his mattress even with the sill. My bed, although it was by the window, was back about three feet.

That night, I readied myself for sleep at about 11:30. All the lights in our house were out, so it definitely looked like no one was home. (Remember, Baron thought I went along on the trip.) Anyway, I was in bed nearly asleep when the light went on in Baron's bedroom. His window was open, and his window shade was up.

I could see into his room perfectly. Baron entered, pulled off his sweater, laid it over a chair, then removed his T-shirt. Sitting on the edge of his bed, with his back to me, he took off his shoes. He then stood up, removed his corduroy jeans, then took off his jockey shorts.

Much to my surprise, he was wearing a snow white swimmer-style jockstrap, a garment that I consider to be the most erotic male apparel ever made. A man wearing one is so beautifully and tantalizing exposed, yet covered, with his bulging pouch holding a "preview of cumming attractions."

Well, there Baron stood, in the middle of his room, watching his reflection in the full-length mirror on his closet door. Soon he was rubbing his hands over his upper arms, massaging and squeezing his nipples, and running the tips of his fingers over his stomach, while his other hand all the while gave plenty of attention to the growing bulge in his jockstrap.

It wasn't very long before his cock, pointing down in the pouch, was trying so hard to stand out straight that it pulled the sides of the pouch away from his body. He then stepped to the chair where his clothes were, got his wallet out of his jeans, and removed something. He then turned off the overhead light and lay on his bed. I thought, "Oh, hell! The show's over." But as soon as he was on the bed, he turned on his bedside lamp.

I could see him perfectly from his nipples to mid-thigh. Lying there on his back with his cock just bulging in the pouch, he did more of the same, playing with his nipples and massaging the jockstrap. Then he lifted up his hips, reached up to the waistband of the jockstrap with both hands and peeled it off, throwing it to where the rest of his clothes were.

His nice and thick cock was uncut and about six and three-quarter inches long. Hard as a rock and pointing up towards his navel, it lay nearly flat against his abdomen. He then leaned away from me and obviously spat in his hand. He rubbed the saliva all over his cock.

Baron lay there, slowly massaging his rock-hard cock. He then put some more spit on it and reached over to the bedside table, picking something up—a little square foil package. At first I didn't know what it was, but he tore it open and took out a rubber. Up till this time, I had never seen one that was new and rolled up, yet I immediately knew what it was.

Baron took the rubber and placed it against the tip of his cock. Now this just absolutely blew my mind. I knew that a rubber was used to screw a girl, so I was totally mystified as to what Baron was doing with it since he was alone. I had never even heard of a boy putting a rubber on to jack off. Anyway, he very slowly rolled it on. Kind of unrolling it with one hand, and sort of pressing his cock with the other. Of course, I know now he was trying to get it on very smooth with no air in it. When it was on, he got a hold of the underside of the band and stretched it down even further. Then, holding his cock straight up, he did the same thing to the top part of the band. He tugged it down even further into the pubic hair, so it was anchored good. Baron, at that point, let go of it with a little snapping sound, a sound that even today can turn me on.

He spit again in his hand and rubbed the saliva all over the outside of the rubber. With the thumb of each hand placed down by the base of his cock, he held his dick straight up like he was admiring it. He had every reason to. The rubber fit flawlessly—not a wrinkle in it—and it was so very transparent. In the light of the lamp it looked like his cock was wrapped in cellophane. It appeared so shiny and glisteny.

Baron then took a hold of it and started one of the most sensuous jack-offs I have ever seen. He took long, slow strokes from the head clear down to the base, then back up to the head. Long, slow strokes. Once in a while he'd speed up, then slacken. At times, he'd remove his hand entirely, as if he was reaching the "about-to-cum" feeling. Then he'd start again and build up.

He must have kept it up for nearly a half hour. I don't know but maybe he took one stroke too many because suddenly I could see his sperm gushing forth.

The cum was instantly trapped by the thin, strong, transparent rubber. It swirled all over the head and part of the shaft. He really put a big load in it, and it was beautiful to not only see his body spasming, but to hear his little moans of pleasure.

When Baron finished shooting off, his young cock was still quite hard. While holding the base of his rubber-encased dick with his right hand, with his left hand he took hold of the tip of the rubber and wiggled it all around. He was apparently enjoying the feeling of the cum between his cockhead and the rubber.

Finally he started to go soft. He then got up and went to his bathroom. I heard his toilet flush. He came back, got into bed, turned out the light and went to sleep.

God, what an experience. I lay there with my hard cock in my hand, just fascinated. Not only did I enjoy watching Baron jack off, but I was spellbound by the rubber. I had never seen one on a cock. I had no idea rubbers fit so tight or were so transparent. I could just imagine how good it must feel to have your warm cum swishing all over the head of your cock. I lay there holding my throbbing cock till I was sure Baron was asleep. Then I quietly crawled out of bed and went to our bathroom and jerked off a tremendous load, reliving what I had just seen.

Needless to say, the next day Baron was surprised and probably embarrassed when he found out I had stayed home. He probably feared I saw his show. To put him at ease, I lied, telling him I had gone to a movie, then a party, and didn't get home till after 2 a.m.

In the meantime, I was going out of my mind. I wanted to get a hold of a rubber so bad, but at that time I didn't know where you bought them, how much they cost, or if they came in different sizes.

After the beach, I was wandering around my house, when I suddenly thought of my brother. He was twenty-five, very good-looking, and probably fucking everything on two legs that was female. So I got a brainstorm of going into his room and ever so carefully going through all his drawers.

I couldn't find any rubbers. I just sat there on his bed close to tears of frustration. I wanted a rubber so bad, I must have been like an addict that needed a fix. Suddenly, I thought he just might have some in the pockets of his clothes, so I rifled through God knows how many pairs of slacks and sports coats.

Finally, inside the breast pocket of his favorite jacket, I found a box of Sheiks that held twelve. It had eight in it. I took one, literally ran to the bathroom, locked the door, and took off every stitch of my clothing.

We had a full-length mirror on the back of the bathroom door. I put the rubber down and tried to do everything I saw

Baron do—much rubbing and squeezing of my nipples, tickling of my abdominals, etc., while giving plenty of attention to my already hard six inches and balls. Soon my cock was throbbing like crazy. So, like Baron, I spit in my hand and rubbed it all over.

Then, with hands trembling, I took the rubber and held it up to my nose and smelled it. (I love the smell.) I even placed it, still rolled up, on the tip of my tongue, getting the inside of it real wet with saliva. Then I placed it against the tip of my cock and rolled it down real slow.

When it was on, I pulled the bottom and upper side of the band down even further and let it go with a snap. Satisfied that it was on perfectly, I stood there with my hands down, my profile to the mirror, and really grooved on the sight of it. I think I could have shot off just looking at myself.

It was a very different sensation. I loved the way it felt. Instead of just feeling pressure where your fingers touch your dick, the tight-fitting rubber gave a clingy, slinky feeling all over the entire surface of my cock. How I loved the way it looked. Spitting in my hand and rubbing the saliva all over the outside surface of the slick rubber, I proceeded to emulate Baron's jack-off technique. Long, slow, sensuous strokes. Very soon I had to take my hand away and let it cool off. I'd slowly built up again, then removed my hand. But I was too turned on and too anxious to see what it felt like to shoot off in to hold back. After only about three, maybe four, minutes I shot.

This, too, was so tremendously different a sensation. It felt a hundred percent better than plain jacking off. Instead of my load flying all over the mirror, it came gushing forth only to be instantly trapped by the tight, thin rubber. The orgasm was so intense and strong that my knees buckled, and I just sank to the floor in front of the mirror while still pumping my boy juice into the end of the rubber.

I just stayed there looking at my reflection in the mirror and played with the layer of warm cum between the rubber and my cockhead. Very soon I was rock hard again. I stood up, and this time I jerked like crazy. Very soon I put another load into the already full rubber. I eventually, very reluctantly, took it off and flushed it down the john. I wanted to save it but I didn't know how to wash it out. From that moment on though, I was hooked on the eroticism of jacking off with rubbers.

—San Diego, California

My Teen Scenes

*E*ver since I can remember, I have had some guy's cock up my ass and loved it. It all started when I was about eight years old with my older cousin, Nathan, who was thirteen. We'd spend the night together almost every weekend. We were very close, and I looked up to him and did almost anything he wanted. For some time he had been sucking my little dick. It tickled and felt good.

One night I reciprocated the act and learned how to suck off my first boy. From that night on, he always tried something new, like rubbing his cock in my ass crack or masturbating with hair oils. Finally, late one night, he applied some type of lubricant to my anus and got a hard-on. He then slowly pushed it in me. At first it hurt, but he was patient and luckily had a small prick. After several nights of trying, he finally succeeded. From that night on I have never stopped. We carried on until he was fifteen and I was ten. His interest in girls split us apart.

I was a very frustrated little boy; my hero wouldn't do it anymore, and I had no idea who to turn to. Then my parents split up, and Mom had to work nights. She hired this older teenage boy to sit with us, me and Rachel, my younger sister. His name was Ollie, and he was very nice to us.

I remember one night I peeked in through the crack in the bathroom door and watched him playing with Rachel. I was jealous, ran off to my room, and cried.

When Ollie came in to tell me to take my bath, I protested. He dragged me into the bathroom and, to my delight, stripped me. I ran out when he turned on the water, making him chase me all through the house. He caught me and wrestled me to the floor. I threw my legs up, and his cock, through his pants, rested against my asshole. He was kind of confused at first, but he didn't mind pressing a little harder against it. Then his hand kind of touched my prick and he started tickling me all over. At my insistence, he removed all his clothing and took a bath with me.

I had seen my daddy's big cock, and his kind of looked the same, but not so big. We both had hard-ons. I asked if I could touch his pee-pee. He agreed. I started jacking him like my cousin, and he got real excited. Ollie started fondling me, too, then he asked if he could kiss it. Of course I agreed, and that was the start of my second relationship with a guy.

By the second week of sitting for us, he'd push the head of

his cock into my ass and jack off. I'd pretend to clean up, but for some reason I dug the cum being in my ass. Ollie was real gentle and never tried to force it all the way up me, but he came pretty close a couple of times. My bratty little sister told Mom that he was touching her privates in the tub. Mom blew her stack, and when he showed up that night all hell broke loose. She asked me if he had touched my penis. I shook my head no. She threatened to call the cops if he ever so much as looked at either of us again. So poor Ollie went on his way.

I could only describe myself then as being very trusting and too horny for my own good. On my twelfth birthday, we all went to an amusement park. I was playing around in the men's room, watching guys taking a pee. This older guy talked me into going into a stall with him. He pulled my shorts and cotton underpants down around my ankles and proceeded to give me a blowjob. I foolishly asked him to push his weenie in my butt. Oh, he did it, too.

I lay across the stall, and he supported me. Then he put some spit between my buns and on his huge dick. Then he fucked me raw. I was used to my fingers and some smaller cocks, but he had a real big dong, and he used my ass like I was an adult. Thankfully, he shot off in a hurry, leaving me to try to patch my sore bleeding ass.

I started crying, and a park employee who had just come in heard me and came to see what was wrong. He opened the stall and saw me with my pants down, covered in drops of blood. Once again Mom freaked out, and the police came out and questioned me.

They made me tell all. I was so embarrassed. My mother was screaming and threatening to sue the park. The police scared the shit out of me. An old doctor came and probed his fingers up my butt, and I had to go see a shrink. They never caught the guy. All they did was traumatize me. If everyone would have just left me alone, let me soak my butt in hot water and get some rest, I would have done okay.

I soon started messing around with my friends after that, shying away from guys too much older than me. It was almost three years before I let someone cornhole me again. There was a kid named Ronnie who I went to school with. We went to his house one afternoon. His brothers had porno books, and we snuck out with them to the tree house and jacked off. I leaned over and sucked him off. He licked my dick, and I masturbated.

The next day we repeated the scene, but this time I got him to screw me in the ass. It had been a long time. After the initial pain wore off, I really enjoyed it.

For being fifteen years old, we really did a lot. Most guys my age were still just rubbing and sucking; not us. Almost every afternoon, we'd sneak off somewhere, and he'd hump me. Once he let me do it to him, but he wasn't used to it, and he was sore for two weeks. Mostly, he would suck me, then I'd spread my legs and let him get on top to jackhammer his four inches of meat. Funny thing, though, he could always make me have what is known as an anal orgasm. Then one day, he told me he didn't want to do it anymore. We got into a fight and went our separate ways. Fifteen and heartbroken again.

As time went on, I began making more gay or bi-friends, mostly just fuck-buddies and the like. I would not get emotionally involved though. Guess I was afraid of being rejected. Girls caught my desires in the ninth grade. I was shy and had a few, but mostly I just wanted some guy to cream in my hole.

When I was seventeen I met Ray; he was a college guy. We met in the park one night. He rented us a motel room, and after conning my mom into believing I was staying at a friend's house, we spent the night really making love. He was so masculine—six feet, one hundred and eighty pounds, blond hair, deep blue eyes and a solid seven-inch love tool.

Ray was a helluva lover. He loved to drive his meat into me and then turn over and fulfill my animal desires. He had not had as much experience in anal sex, but was a good learner. I'd skip school, and we would sixty-nine until his roommate got home. Then we would party all night. Usually on the way home, I'd perform fellatio on him in his Triumph, going down the freeway.

Ray dated girls some, and one in particular named Angel got off on group sex with bi-guys. She was beautiful.

Angel got us drunk one night, then pulled both our pricks out and started sucking us. A mouth is a mouth, and I got turned on. We were told to strip, and we did. Soon all three of us were tangled on the floor.

I was a virgin with girls, and she promised to deflower me if I'd suck Ray off. I played along and pretended I had never done such a thing. She guided me down on Ray's pole. Then got him to do the same to me. If she would have only known. We ate her out, and she gave a hell of a good blow herself. I was aching by the time she suggested I eat her while Ray bumfucked me. Playing along, I protested. Finally I entered her cunt and Ray entered my butt. Wow, what a night that was.

—*Tarrant, Texas*

A Cowboy Called Wang

S ince I was ten, I've been living with my uncle and aunt on a ranch. One of my duties was to take care of the leather tack and saddles, which were kept in a room running the length of the cowhands' bunkhouse.

Curious about sex, I soon made a number of peepholes at various places in the stalls, so that I could observe the cowboys whenever I wanted to.

Often I would catch one or two of them beating off under the sheets, when they thought no one was paying attention.

Sometimes the older cowboys would take advantage of a greenhorn when he first came to work with us. The first day out on the range, the new guy inevitably would be tired and saddle sore. That night the older hands would sit around drinking, making sure the greenhorn got completely tanked up. When he didn't know what he was doing and couldn't have done anything anyway, they would pull down his pants and bum-fuck him one after another until they'd each had a turn. Then they'd just button him up again and leave him to sleep it off fully clothed on the bunk.

One of the most interesting regular cowboys with us was a guy called Wang. The nickname was aptly descriptive, because Wang had managed to get his cock sucked by almost every guy in the county, straight or whatever. He was famous for the size of his dick. It was really long, but quite slim with the last four inches or so taking a decided dip down. This made him really easy to swallow.

Because of his renown for having such a long prick, guys always wanted him to prove it. (If you ride horses for a living, you just don't let any of your equipment hang down the inside of your pants' leg, believe me.) So he would make a bet with them.

The beer glasses out here are big ones, and traditionally they are tall. Wang would agree to show his prick to a guy, but only on the condition that he would stuff it into a full glass of beer. He would catch the displaced beer in his own glass and would get to drink that. But the catch was that if Wang managed to touch the bottom of the glass with the head of his prick, the other guy had to agree to lick or suck the beer off Wang's tool—to suck him dry in other words. Most guys agreed to the challenge, because no one figured that a guy's dink could be long enough to touch the bottom of one of those glasses. Anyway, they figured the cold beer would probably stop Wang from getting a real hard-on. They were fooled every time, and like I say, almost every guy in the county had tasted Wang's beer-covered tool.

Actually, Wang got the best end of the deal in other ways, too. For one thing, because he was shaped so long and thin, he could usually slip it into a guy's mouth and right down his throat before the guy knew what was happening. Also, I suspect that Wang was a real exhibitionist. Because when he did this trick, any observer could tell from the look in his eyes and the surge in his loins that he was actually shooting his load. Again, the guy who was doing the sucking, especially if he was straight, would probably not notice because the cum went straight down his throat. It never had the chance to fill his mouth up. It was only as Wang pulled his long organ out, that the suckee would get a taste of the last thick drops of cum, then he'd realize what had happened.

A couple of years ago I observed this challenge through one of the holes I'd cut in the bunkhouse wall. The new guy was a little fellow named Gary. All the other cowboys stood around watching as he took the challenge. But one thing I noticed was that he seemed to be massaging Wang's cock with his throat while it was all the way in there.

About a week later, while the other hands were in the living area playing cards, I was at one of my peepholes when I saw Wang and Gary together. Gary complimented Wang on the size of his tool and said it wouldn't have to be covered with beer next time, if he wanted him to take it. Wang replied that he had liked the feel of Gary's mouth, and what about now?

So Wang whipped his tool out, and they started into a real face-fucking session. Wang certainly wasn't quick this time, and Gary was going down and swallowing every inch available. Then they noticed that the other cowboys had come to the door and were watching, all of them rubbing their crotches. One had even taken his prick out and was giving himself a hand-job. Well, Wang just shot his load right then

As he pulled out, the guy who was jerking himself moved in and said he wanted some of that action, too. Gary had to oblige, and the others started getting ready for their turn. Gary obviously knew what he was doing because each of them ended up blowing his load with a real gasp of pleasure. I went around to the door and stood in line, too. That is how I lost my virginity and had my first real-man blowjob.
                                                    —*Haskell, Texas*

135

Ranch Raunch

B Y   A L   S K A N D E R

W hen I was growing up, my family lived on a ranch where there was always a great deal of work to do. I always enjoyed my chores, although both of my brothers could hardly wait to grow up and move away from the ranch. Neither of them seemed attracted to that way of life. But all of us pitched in, and our spread was one the whole family could be proud of.

Then, when I was sixteen, my father died. For a while, it looked like we would have to sell the ranch. Both of my brothers had left home and were in college. I was still in high school, and with only Mom and myself, we never had enough time to get all the work done. She thought we should sell out and move to the city, but I kept arguing and pleading with her. I hated the idea that we might have to give up the family homestead. I think Mom felt the same way I did, because eventually she let herself be talked into hiring a man to help us with the chores.

His name was Jenner and he was twenty-five years old. He worked a long and hard day, always being quietly efficient and always knowing what to do next without having to be told. He was as country-oriented as I was, and loved ranching. Mom quickly learned she could really count on him, and soon she stopped thinking about selling the ranch. Meanwhile, I grew closer to Jenner than I had ever been to my real brothers.

For the first few weeks, Jenner lived in the tack room of the stable. But soon we came to feel so much like family that it only seemed natural to invite him to live in the house with Mom and me. Besides, summer was coming and the house was air conditioned. The tack room was not. So Jenner moved his things into my room, making me feel like I had a new brother to share things with.

From the first, Jenner presented himself as a person who was sure of himself. He never hesitated, he never looked self-conscious, he never wavered in indecision, and he managed this self-control with one of the mildest attitudes I had ever seen. Jenner was shy. But he was also bold. He taught me a great deal.

The first night he spent in my room was a revelation in itself. I was bent over my desk, doing homework when he walked in, fresh from the shower. He was wearing his towel around his waist and his long, sun-bleached hair was still dripping onto his shoulders. I looked up, nodded, and went back to work.

"What're you writing, Bud?" he asked in that soft voice of his.

"Just a paper that's not very interesting."

"What do you mean 'not very interesting'? What's it about?" And he walked over to stand at my shoulder, reading over it. He read silently until he noticed that his hair was dripping on me.

"Sorry about that, kid," he said, taking the towel from around his waist and drying his hair more thoroughly while continuing to read.

The proximity of his nakedness made me really uncomfortable. Knowing he was standing only inches away, I took pains not to look at him. I bent lower over my work. He probably sensed my discomfort, because he moved away and lay on his bed. After a few minutes he spoke again.

"Bud?"

I swiveled in my chair to face him.

"Are you going to take over this ranch next year, or are you going away to school? It was a subject I had thought about for many weeks. It deserved a good honest answer. But all I could think of at the moment was the fact that he still hadn't put on any clothes. I was careful to look him in the eye, but my peripheral vision took in his whole body—a great muscular, tanned form lying on its back with its head propped up on a pillow.

"I want to stay here, and Mom needs the help," I managed to say, "but the teachers and counselor at school think I shouldn't put off taking a degree." He nodded understanding. "Besides, if I don't take the scholarship next year, I don't know if they'll offer it to me again."

"Yeah, it's tough trying to decide." While we talked on, his eyes would move here and there, always returning to mine to make a point or listen closely to what I was saying. But my eyes stayed on his face. I think he noticed this and figured out the problem.

"Tell me something, Bud. Does it bother you, my not wearing a robe or something?"

"Of course not!" I think my face must have reddened, but my eyes stayed glued to his. "I've been in gym classes all my life. Why should it matter?" I feigned nonchalance. What I didn't tell him was that my brothers and I had never been naked around one another. I had never seen my father undressed. I never even saw my mother in a nightgown. But I tried hard to appear cool.

"I usually sleep in pajamas," I cracked. "Is that going to bother you?"

"I'll get used to it." He smiled a warm smile. "Good night, Bud. Thanks for sharing your room with me." He pulled the sheet over himself, turned out the bedside light, and rolled onto his side to sleep. I went back to work.

That set the pattern of our night-time conversations. We would always discuss my future and what I thought I wanted out of life. Somehow, during these talks, Jenner became my idol. He never said anything especially profound or did anything superhuman, but the quiet consistency of his work and his ever-smiling attitude became attributes I wanted to acquire. I even became easy with his nudity. As the days progressed, I felt comfortable enough to let my gaze wander over him as he lay prone on the bed. His physique was really remarkable and, I'm sure, added to my hero worship. The long hours working at ranch routine gave him muscular arms and a powerful chest. His waist was thin, and his stomach had a washboard effect. He had long legs with especially strong thighs from many hours in the saddle. All in all, it was a body I could wish for myself.

Jenner never seemed to mind that I spent long moments looking at his body. Most of the time he didn't seem to notice. And when he did, it was just in passing, and he never called my attention to it by word or glance. Ours was a nice easygoing relationship.

I did feel like a voyeur every morning, however. I would always wake ahead of Jenner and the alarm clock. In the first light of the sun, I would lie in bed and watch him sleep. He slept in every possible position. And every morning, without fail, he had a huge erection.

I had never seen a man's erection before. Except my own, of course. Jenner was built much bigger than me, and the sight of his cock, erect and bobbing in pendulous hugeness, always filled me with a sort of a vague envy as well as a vaguer stimulation. Sometimes I got hard just looking at him.

One morning I awoke to find Jenner lying on his back, sprawled half off the bed with his top sheet strewn off the footboard. His cock was stretching and waving toward the ceiling. I had awakened with a hard-on of my own, and found myself grinding it between my stomach and the mattress, looking at his body across the room. Unthinking and not fully conscious, I continued rubbing against the sheet until I was very near coming. Then I saw that he was awake and watching me. I froze. Our eyes met. I hopped off the bed and aimed for the door to the hallway bathroom. He hopped up at the same time and grinned at me.

"Good morning. I see you woke up with the same idea I did." And he gestured toward my pajama bottoms, which were tenting outward. He quickly stepped into a pair of underwear and jammed his erection into it. Wrapping a towel around his waist—I'm sure for my mother's benefit, in case she was up—he pretended to wrestle me toward the door.

"I'll race you for the cold shower." And he half raced and half pushed me down the hall to the bathroom, both of us laughing and feeling good.

"You go ahead first," he said as he closed the bathroom door behind us. "I'll shave." He turned to the sink and started getting out his lather, blade, and so on. I stripped off my pajamas and got in the shower. I always take a hot shower, no matter what. I did that morning, too. As the steam started to fill his shaving mirror, he called to me.

"Hey, I thought you needed a *cold* shower." And he laughed. I could hear the squeaking as he rubbed the mirror. I lathered all over and looked down at myself. My erection had softened a little.

"Hey yourself, " I called. "I thought *you* needed a cold shower." I splashed water over the curtain at him. Before I knew what had happened, a hand came through the curtain and turned the water setting to the coldest temperature. I howled and grabbed at the faucet with one hand, and at his hand with the other. We fought with the faucet until the curtain was half-open and water was all over the floor. As we wrestled, I got him into a headlock and forced his face under the shower's stream. He was laughing.

"I give up. I give up," he said, gasping. With that, he stepped into the bathtub and closed the curtain, straightening up under the gush of water. I had released my hold on him, and my arms were sort of sliding down from around his neck. He was still wearing his underwear, now soaked, but by his closeness I could feel that his erection had not subsided at all. It pulsed against mine. I dropped my arms and moved away from him. Jenner turned into the spray of water and stripped off his jockey shorts.

"I guess I don't need these in here," he laughed. As he stood with his back to me, I looked closely at his muscles, his tan line, the smooth roundness of his ass. I wanted to touch him badly. Without turning around, Jenner spoke.

"Wash my back?" he asked in a low voice. I hesitated and then reached for the soap. Working up a lather, I stroked his shoulders and the backs of his arms, his strong shoulder blades, and the small of his back. There I stopped. I let my hands rest at his waist and slowly I leaned my forehead in against his neck.

"Don't stop, Bud," he murmured as the water splashed down about our heads. "Keep going. It feels good."

I worked my hand slowly down to his hips, rubbing in small circles. He twisted his head to speak right into my ear.

"You've wanted to touch me for a long time. It's okay." At those words I felt something release inside of me. I knew what I wanted, and I knew that what I wanted was really okay.

I let one hand move around to Jenner's stomach, circling just above his pubic hair. My other hand circled onto his ass and felt the hard muscles packed into those orbs. My hand drew the line of the fold in his ass many times, working deeper and deeper with every pass, until my hand was reaching between his legs, tickling the bag that contained his testicles. Jenner moved his legs, spreading them.

I responded, pressing my stomach along the length of his side. Jenner put one arm around my waist as he submitted to my touch and curiosity. My own cock stretched across Jenner's stomach. As one hand fondled his balls from behind, my other traced the lines on the horsecock stretching out before me. Both of us watched my fingers run up and down his cock, pressing it this way and that. Then I grasped it, first exerting pressure and then releasing it. Jenner moaned and closed his eyes.

I had never felt this for a man before. Never even fantasized about it. But as both of my hands kept busy massaging and stroking, I leaned my lips to his cheek and kissed him lightly. He smiled and moved his head, making my next peck an off-center mouth-to-mouth. I leaned forward an inch more and we kissed for real.

As the water splashed about our bodies, our arms brought us into an embrace. Our erect cocks were pressed between our bellies. We kissed deeply and ground our stomachs together, breathing heavily. Hands found asses. Tongues found tonsils. Cocks found stimulation until we both shuddered into orgasm almost simultaneously, clutching at each other's bodies there in the shower.

It took several moments for us to recover. Smiling broad smiles of contentment, we splashed each other's stomachs and hurried to complete our showers and shaves. We could smell breakfast waiting.

Jenner and I settled into a routine of sex. Almost every night we would discover and re-discover each other's bodies. And he would let me look and touch, to my heart's content, even when neither of us was really in the mood for a heavy session. When summer came and I was out of school, Jenner and I found lots of time to explore each other out of doors. I'll never forget the first day I ever tried oral sex.

We'd been herding a few strays back into their pasture and had finally completed the task. Jenner suggested a quick dip in the pond before we went back to the house for supper. Under the blue of a clear sky, we tethered the horses and stripped our clothes away, exhilarating in the feel of the breeze on our naked skin. As always, just seeing him excited me. Watching him stretch his legs and arms, bending this way and that, my cock grew erect immediately. He noticed and smiled. We walked down to the pond and dove in. After a few minutes of energetic swimming, we both settled on a little grassy area nearby.

Jenner stretched out on his stomach and I lay on my side next to him. I stroked his back from his neck to his thighs several times before he responded by gyrating his hips slightly. Then he turned over to expose his fully aroused cock. I put my head on Jenner's stomach and watched my hand at close range as it played with that giant tumescence — probing, stroking, and teasing it.

"Use your tongue on me, Bud," Jenner said. The tone made it a request. I continued playing with his cock, thinking. Then I shifted a little closer and let my tongue play out and lick the very tip of his cock. Mmmm, I couldn't tell what I was smelling or tasting, but I knew I liked it. I let my tongue lick around the blood-engorged head.

Jenner moaned and his hips began a gentle rocking motion. Trying it out, I rose above him and let the end of his cock find its way into my mouth. He rocked and moved it slowly in and out, while I balanced above, accommodating his movements as best I could.

Almost immediately he pulled my head away from his cock. I could see he was about to come. Instinctively I pulled my head free from his hand and went down on his cock as far as I could go, sucking his cum in spurts. Jenner gasped, his legs spasmed, and his hands grasped my head to him as he climaxed more powerfully than I had ever seen him do before.

And so Jenner and I added a new element to our lovemaking, as eventually we added so many others.

Time passed and Mom decided to move to her sister's. I think it was too hard for her, living on the ranch after Dad left us. I never went away to school, of course. Jenner and I continued to happily run the ranch for years. Together. Then, the summer I turned twenty-four, Jenner was killed in an accident.

My life was never the same afterward. Oh, I coped. I met new people and even wound up having another lover. Still, I treasure the memory of those early years. I learned an awful lot.

"I Was The Last Patient That Day"

I would like to tell you and your readers of an experience I had a few years ago when I was living in Los Angeles. I had applied for a job as a construction worker and I needed to take a pre-employment physical in order to qualify.

Arriving at the doctor's office late in the afternoon, I was the last patient scheduled to see him that day. He was a good-looking Japanese fellow about my age (early thirties), very friendly and outgoing. After greeting me with a warm handshake, he gave his pretty blonde nurse the rest of the day off, saying that he could handle my examination alone.

He led me into his office where he took my medical history, and asked me some friendly questions about family, work, etc. We then went into the examining room where he told me to strip "bareass naked" and get on the scale.

He watched as I undressed, commenting on the amount of hair on my chest, back and ass, and complimenting me on the size of my pecker, saying that my girlfriend was a very lucky woman. I felt flattered by his words and was also starting to get turned on. It took a lot of effort on my part not to throw a hard-on right then and there.

When he was through weighing me, he slapped me on the butt and told me to sit on the examining table. He then took my blood pressure, examined my eyes, ears, nose and throat, and listened to my breathing with a stethoscope. Afterwards, he put on his rubber gloves and proceeded to get down to serious business. He had me stand at attention, and told me to cough while he probed my groin to check for a hernia. When he retracted my foreskin, I couldn't help myself any longer and felt my cock growing hard in his hand. He laughed, telling me that it was a normal reaction and not to be embarrassed because, after all, we were both men.

He then suddenly remembered that he had forgotten to take my temperature, and asked me if I would mind having it taken rectally since this was the quickest and most accurate method. At this point, I was really beginning to enjoy myself and gladly bent over the table with my ass in the air, while he smeared a dab of K-Y gel on the bulb of the thermometer.

My dong became rock hard when he spread my ass cheeks apart and inserted that glass rod in my asshole. After withdrawing the thermometer, he told me not to move because he wanted to check out my prostate gland. After feeling his fingers up my ass, I felt like a stallion in heat and was sporting an eight-inch boner when he told me to stand up.

By this time, he was displaying quite a bulge in his own trousers and, grinning, asked me if I would like any help in getting rid of my hard-on. Would I! He was out of his clothes like a shot, and for the next hour we took turns sucking and fucking each other on the large, comfortable couch in his adjoining office.

Afterwards, we sat there naked, talking, when I happened to mention that I had wanted to be a doctor when I was a kid, but that my grades weren't good enough to cut the mustard. He told me that he would be able to show me how to perform a physical examination using himself as the guinea pig. I then carried out the same procedure on him that he had done to me a few minutes before, with him acting as both instructor and patient. This got us so hot that we got it on one more time on the carpeted floor of the examining room.

After that, we became good buddies as well as sexual partners, and continued to see each other until I moved away about a year ago. I would like to hear from any of your readers who have had similar experiences. Even now, the sight of a masculine guy in doctor's garb makes my organ throb.

Rapid City, South Dakota

"Deryk Had Muscular Arms, Big Pecs..."

Y our article on straight men prompted me to write of my experience with a guy who from all outward signs only had women on his mind. Since then I have discovered you never can tell.

Deryk was eighteen, I twenty, when we met at my parents' house. My sister was giving a party and Deryk was her boyfriend's best friend who I had only heard about, but never seen. From all the talk with my sister's girlfriends, I couldn't wait.

I was still swimming in our back yard doing some one-arm butterflies, when out of the corner of my eye I saw this guy standing on the balcony looking at me. I knew it wasn't Keith, so it had to be Deryk. Not paying attention, I forgot how close the wall was and crashed into it—a clank you could hear in the house. As I pulled myself out of the pool, the guy on the balcony came running out of the house to see if I was okay. I was fine, of course, but decided to see what he would do. "I don't know," I said. He proceeded to give me little feels all over.

"Who are you?" I asked. He then looked me right in the eyes and said, "I'm Deryk. You must be Roger." He offered his hand to me to shake.

"Are you ever good-looking!" He was, too. He was about 5'10" tall and weighed about 150 pounds, with layered, chocolate brown hair, brown eyes with long eyelashes, an incredible mouth and nose, thick neck, muscular arms, and under his tight T-shirt, nice big pectorals and a washboard stomach. His shorts were packed nicely, and those legs! Well, I was getting a little weak from all this, so I said I'd better go lie down in the poolhouse. He followed me in and asked if I would like a drink or something. I said I was okay and started to get out of my bathing suit. With my back to him, I looked into the bar. The reflection showed him giving my ass the once-over, then the twice-over.

"Yeah, you look all right," he said, heading back to the house. My heart was pounding, and I did lie down. Over the next few weeks, Deryk was at our house quite a bit with whatever girlfriend he had that day, sunning or playing tennis. I would always get the feeling of being stared at when he visited, so one day I got my ex-girlfriend to come over to watch him while I swam. She told me he definitely had the hots for me. He even rubbed his crotch now and then while staring at my backside. Okay!

Deryk knew I swam from five to six every day, then put some Pink Floyd on, got high, and lay in the poolhouse till my heartrate went down. So, when he came by alone one day at five-thirty and I wasn't in the pool, he headed over to the poolhouse to find me. I still wasn't really sure about him, but I was ready—lying face down on the daybed with the covers across my thighs, my bare ass exposed.

I heard him come up the flagstone steps and could see in the bar mirrors. He stopped and stared at my ass intently for a while, then adjusted his crotch a few times due to his cock getting hard. I was hard as a rock from watching him, but pretended I was fast asleep. He came over and called to me, then shook my shoulders trying to wake me. When he got no response, I guess he felt he could take some liberties. Right then, he ran his hand from my shoulder down my back to my ass and then down to feel my thighs. Being a swimmer, these areas are quite firm. He gave a little moan as his hand went back to my ass again, squeezing my cheeks and running his fingers into my crack, then to my balls.

Well, this had gone far enough to convince me that sex with Deryk was not going to be any one-way street with me doing the work (i.e., sucking him off like the few other straight guys I had wasted my time on).

I gave a little groan, and he pulled his hand away quickly as I rolled over on my back, my seven and a half inches staring him in the face.

"Hi, Deryk," I said, smiling up at him and rubbing his leg. "Your hands sure felt good on me."

"You felt good on my hands," he replied as he sat next to me on the bed.

"Do you want to take this further?" I asked. "You know I do, don't you?"

I told him about the other straight guys I had been with (one he even knew), but he said not to worry about that. To prove it, he leaned over and stuck his tongue in my mouth. (Straight guys will sometimes even let you fuck them, but kissing is definitely a no-no.)

He loved to neck as I do, too. It was quite intense—our teeth sometimes clicking together. He then proceeded to work me over so good, actually just like a guy would a chick, which he thought must work as I was only the second guy he had been with.

We necked then, and he sucked my neck, shoulders, and pectorals, driving me wild. He then sucked my cock all the way down and all around for twenty minutes. Then he dove on my balls, tonguing them slowly.

Then came the shock as he flipped me over on my stomach and proceeded to give my ass the best tongue-lashing of all time. He was moaning, groaning, and getting right into it. Then he started to finger my ass, and without stopping our necking, put his eight-inch cock into me. He fucked me for quite a while. Then he pulled my legs wide apart and watched as his cock went in and out of my ass. Shortly he pulled out and went down on me again, sucking my balls and pushing his tongue into my ass. I was so far gone, it was unreal.

Next he flipped me over and started rubbing his cock along my crack as I pushed back. He started alternating fucking me and rubbing his cock on my cheeks, all the time telling me my ass is the most amazing thing he'd ever seen, and the tightest thing he'd ever fucked. I rolled over and lifted my legs. He started pounding real hard into me. I couldn't take any more and shot cum. It flew everywhere. Seeing that, he couldn't take any more and shot his cum in me, bucking and moaning and pushing his tongue in my mouth.

We still see each other for sex, but due to peer pressure he still fucks girls and has a girlfriend. But I get the best of him. (By the way, I'm twenty-seven now.) He also likes to get his ass sucked, fucked, and sucked again. He even pulls his cheeks apart for me, which looks so hot I go at him like crazy. He even comes from me just sucking his ass and balls. Too hot!

My boyfriends usually don't believe me when I tell them about him, because his deep voice, looks, and actions don't give him away at all. My last lover and I split because he walked in on us—with Deryk's head buried between my ass-cheeks and I on my stomach.

—*Canada*

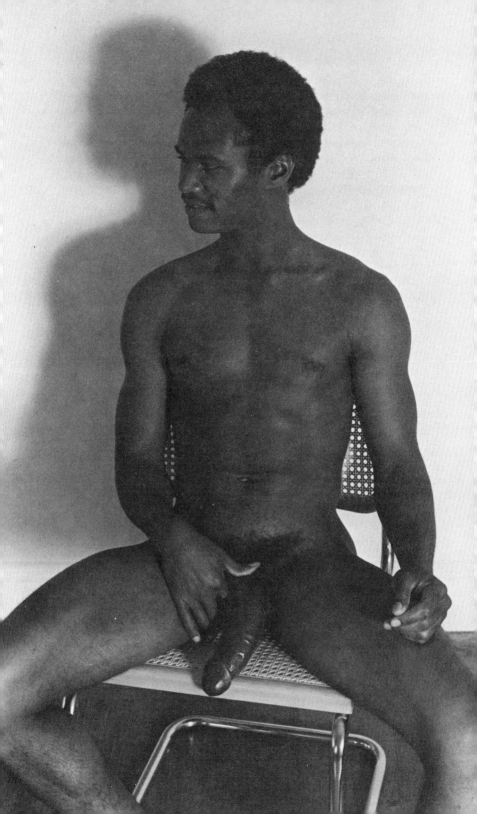

"I Wrestled A long, Black Cock From His Levis"

Two weeks ago Ed, the owner and manager of my apartment house, hired a new maintenance man for the four-story, 35-apartment setup I live in. Ed had a friend in Indianapolis who knew a black guy who lost his job when the building he worked in burned down. Could Ed give this guy a job? Since maintenance workers are hard to find these days, Ed got rid of the lazy bastard who was here and took on Ezra. I guess the pay isn't so hot, but there's a nice little apartment in the basement that goes with it—a pretty good deal for the times.

So, two weeks ago, Ezra arrived—tall, very dark and pretty good-looking. He is maybe thirty or so with a little gray here and there in his jet-black, curly hair. There are few blacks in this town, and my pulse gave a jump when Ed took him around to meet us all.

"Ezra here will take care of all the problems of the place," said Ed. "He's a good man. You treat him good; he'll treat you good." Ezra shook hands with me, and that big hand squeezing mine gave me a thrill. If he only knew I was undressing his big physique with my eyes.

After that I saw him a few times now and then. He surely was a worker and kept the place up fine. But every time I saw him, my dick tingled.

Last Saturday evening when I came home from the filling station/garage I own here, I found water on the floor near my sink in the kitchen. A fucken leak! Was the downstairs guy in? I wondered. I called. His deep voice answered. He'd come right up. I'm on the first floor. In about five minutes he was there with his tool kit (and with his *tool,* too, which I never saw but wished I could).

He's a very pleasant guy and got right down to business, opening the lower door, sliding himself on his back under the sink, and working on the pipes. With his long Levi-clad legs extended, my eyes, as they always do, surveyed the crotch. With the cloth pulled tight, what lay under the cloth bulged most dramatically! This was a MAN! My mind pictured what lay darkly under that denim. My lust for colored guys lifted up my pants. Oh, how I wanted to get on the floor and go after him.

I made some coffee, and it had finished perking by the time

the pipe was fixed and Ezra crawled out. Sure, he'd have some coffee and a roll. He didn't mind staying a little while to chew the fat. He seemed to appreciate my friendliness and interest in him. We sat at the table and talked. He said he was sure glad to get the job. Jobs were mighty scarce where he came from. Did he have a family there? No more. His wife and two kids left him and moved back South.

"Guess I gave her a bad time," he said.

"Yeah?"

He gave a little apologetic grin. "Got tired of me fuckin' around," he said.

"That isn't so easy here," I said. "Not many blacks around this town."

"Shit," he said. "Black or white, I ain't particular, but I see what you mean. Ain't seen, so far, any gash that'd let me in. Know any that needs a good sportin' man?" His fine white teeth showed in a grin. I confessed I didn't.

"Well," said Ezra, "until I can get a little time off to get to the city, guess I'll just have to make do!"

I looked at his dark hand and pictured what it must often fist . . . and damn, I had to control myself to not lick my lips.

Two days later my rent was due. "Pay it to the new man," Ed had said. so, check in hand, I went down to big Ezra's domain. He wasn't in the furnace room or the locker setup, so I knocked at the door of his small apartment in the southeast corner. His deep voice responded and he opened his door. There he stood, a magnificent study in ebony, broad, bare-chested, and Levi-clad. He welcomed me in when I handed him the check. It was obvious we liked each other.

His place was simply furnished and neat. On the wall, near his unmade bed, I could see through the partly open door some most revealing "girly" pictures—white and black ladies showing what must have been, to him, sensational tits and "gash." That Ezra had the hots for them was evident; they were the inspiration for his big dark fist.

"How ya doin'?" I asked. "Like the job?"

"Sure. Fine," was his response. "Just gotta few problems. Kinda lonely sometimes, know what I mean?"

"Yeah," I said. I watched that big hand of his make a fist and move it up and down.

"I wind up keeping this big fist workin' hard!"

Boldly I said, "It doesn't have to."

"No?" His big dark eyes looked at me with interest. "Got some babes for me . . . or somethin' . . . ?"

I gave a most blatant stare at his crotch. "Maybe you wouldn't be interested . . ."

"Interested? Shit, yes." He could see I was interested. His big hand went to the V of his pants and caressed his crotch.

"There are other good ways . . ." I said.

"Yeah," said Ezra. "Anybody want somethin' I got down there they're more'n welcome. Maybe you."

With that invitation, I got up from my chair, went to him, and placed my right hand on the hiding place. Something big and hot was under that cloth. "I been wonderin'," said the big guy grinning.

My hand was at the top of the zipper; I pulled it down. Ezra obligingly spread his legs wide when my hand went in to touch his hot responding flesh. My tongue came out while I wrestled a beautiful, long, black cock out of those Levi's. Huge! Long extended! Glossy black with the foreskin slowly peeling back. Perfect to be put to use.

"A big bastard, eh?" said Ezra. "Maybe too much?"

"No problem, I think," I said. "What a wondeful wang!"

"You wanta hot suck on it?" asked the big stud. He stood up and shed his Levi's. What a masterpiece of man. He went to the door and locked it, with that long, stiff mouthpiece swaying and the long hanging man-bag bouncing. "Come on the bed," said my black quarry. Oh how he needed me.

And on those white sheets, I was all over that very dark body. On fire with lust for him, my tongue was athletically exploring all over. What a chest. What taut, upstanding nipples! What a hard washboard belly! What a forest of thick, wiry, glinting curls! What a heavy ball-bearing bag holding his goodies! What a soaring, throbbing cock. I was after it! My jaws were spread at their widest to initially get in the very wide, flared, glossy cockhead. Then I relaxed a little as his delectable hot meat slid in—deep! Deep! I got my head comfortably in position, my throat calm, and began the age-old cocksucking ritual.

Ezra felt so huge in me but so wonderful. He patted my slowly moving head with contentment in response to my hot, gripping suction. It was evident he was a long-laster, but I had been sucking him so long, he was close to the shooting point when there was a rap on the outer door. Ezra took his cock from me, sleek and slippery, and grunted, "Shit!" "My check for the rent," said a woman's voice.

"Okay. Thanks. Slide it under the door," said my man. That done, looking so male, the big, black, wonderful guy strode back to bed, took my head in both hands and thrust back full length into me again. "Wonderful!" I thought, giving a grunt. Now there was added sucking time to get him to the peak again. More time to fondle, caress, and play with that fat, heavy pouch that held the gift he was to give me. My head rose and fell. My tongue thrashed. I brought the glans up to my clasping lips, licked the slipperiness there, and then plunged down full-length, letting his wiry curls tickle my nose. Then gently I bit my way up the full length until my pointed tongue could slide in a little way into the parted cock-lips oozing "lube." I then slid slowly down the pulsing prodigious length to a steady up, down, up, down rhythm again. Grunts of deep pleasure came from big Ezra.

It was a while before I heard increased deep breathing and little ecstatic moans from the big guy under me. Then "HERE, BABY! HERE SHE BLOWS!" Ezra triggered his gun, and how that gun of his could shoot. I had to lift up a ways on it not to get strangled by his man juice, but still, as every skilled cock-sucker does, I kept up the up-down motion as his hot cream zinged out. Thick, rich, full-bodied, copious, he sent it into me. I gulped, swallowed, and was determined to keep some in my cheeks to savor the fruit of Ezra's loins. When had I ever enjoyed a cock so much?

When he was out of my mouth, his cock flopped over his right thigh, still throbbing and softening only a little. I licked over it, tongued it, getting all there was left to get of that rich, tasty semen. I could see him eyeing up the pictures on the wall, those tits and cunts, previous inspiration for his fist, his sex need.

"No woman ever liked that dick of mine as much as you," he whispered. "Wow, you really emptied those hot balls of mine!" He patted my sweaty head in ardent gratitude.

I felt up the warmth of his lovely pouch. "This doesn't feel empty to me," I said. I slid the still full-bodied hard nuts around in the bag.

"They'll fill up again fast," said Ezra encouragingly.

"I sure hope so."

Ezra grabbed my clothed body tightly against his dark nakedness. His wide lips planted a kiss on my cheek, but I, wanting those lips against mine, parted his lips with my tongue and he let me in. I doubt that he'd ever had the taste of his own cum, but he got it that time. And with vigor, he cleaned my stiff tongue.

"Jeez, you're sure handy to have around," said my maintenance man. "I sure could use you often."

I grabbed his big, right hand, tickling the rough palm. "Your fist has pleasured that luscious big thing of yours for the last time," I said.

"If you want my big fucker you're going to get it," Ezra said, pulling me tightly against him. My head went to his wide dark chest, my lips opened and surrounded a taut nipple. I nursed it for a while, while he held my head down tight to it. "You do that just too much and you gonna get somethin' much bigger in yer puss again. Come on, you sweet cocksucker, get down on it again!"

And did I! That bag of his held a great deal of man-honey, and his second cumming was as plentiful and good as the first.

Well, that was our first sex-encounter and it's been repeated, and repeated, with even more pleasure for both of us every time. We both get what we need and we both couldn't have it better.

—*New Rockford, North Dakota*

"You're tough . . . you're macho . . . and the most respected longshoreman around. But let's face it, Dirk, you have a crush on Boy George."

Nighttime Janitor

When I was a senior in high school, I got a summer job working as a nighttime janitor at a doctor's office.

At the time, I knew I was gay, but except for some mutual jack-offs, I'd never been able to do with a man what I really wanted to do—fuck and suck.

Anyway, one evening during my first week of work, I was surprised when I unlocked the office to find the lights on and to hear someone in one of the examining rooms. I was even more surprised when I went to investigate and found it was Jim, the x-ray technician who worked for the doctor. Jim was twenty-six, single, and the best-looking man I had ever seen in my life. I had met him when I was interviewed for the job, but hadn't seen him since. He usually went out to the hospital around three o'clock, and was long gone by the time I came to clean at seven.

When I'd met him for the first time, I almost came in my pants. He was about six feet tall and built like an Adonis, with longish brown hair, well-cut and squeaky clean looking. His face was like a painting—really almost too pretty to be true—with perfect, straight white teeth and the most beautiful eyes which were sort of bluish grey, clear, and deep. He was really not believable. And on top of gorgeous, he was friendly.

So, when I found him in the examining room I got really flustered, and could hardly talk.

"Hey, I didn't mean to scare you," he said. "I've been wanting to clean these cabinets for months. Now I finally got a night off, so I have my chance."

I muttered something and went down the hall to the janitor's closet to get the mop and bucket. All the while I mopped, I kept trying to think of something to talk to him about. He tried to get a conversation going a couple of times, but I was totally tongue-tied.

Finishing the rooms, except for the one he was in, I was mopping the hall when he said, "Hey, you're quick. You ought to take a break."

"Yeah, I will when I finish the hall."

"No, no, I insist," he said. "Come on in here, sit down, and tell me about school and tennis." He remembered I like to play tennis.

"Oh, school's okay," I said, "but since I took this job I really don't have much time for tennis."

"Too bad," he replied. "I know what you mean though. I'm so busy with work, it seems like I rush to work, rush to the hospital, rush home, and then start all over again. I don't even have time to get a hard-on." He laughed and watched my reaction—a very deep blush. "You know what I mean," he said, "no time for anything."

"Yeah," I stammered, "but you must like your work though; you're so busy all the time."

"It's okay," he replied.

He was moving instruments in and out of the cabinet, and for lack of anything else to talk about I kept asking what the instruments were, how they worked, and stuff like that. He would tell me and show me how they worked. When Jim showed me a huge needle used for draining cysts, I said I'd hate to have that used on me. "It would hurt so much."

He laughed and said, "No, here's what would hurt." He pulled a long chrome tube from the cabinet that looked like a dildo. "Know what it is?"

"NO!"

"It's called a proctoscope. It's used for looking up the rectum. They grease it real good first, but sometimes it still hurts. At least usually. I guess there are those who like it." He wiggled his eyebrows like Groucho Marx and laughed. He handed the proctoscope to me.

"This is a finger cot," he said, handing me a rolled-up rubber that looked like a condom. "The doctor uses this on his finger when he does a rectal exam, or else he uses rubber gloves."

"Yeah, I know about that," I said. "I had a physical for the tennis team, and the doctor did that to me."

"Fun, huh?" he laughed and wiggled his eyebrows again.

"Oh, sure," I replied as sarcastic as I could.

"Well, give me that stuff back. I'm finished," he said.

I gave him the stuff and tried desperately to think of something to keep him there. "What's this?" I asked pointing to the stirrup on the examining table, even though I knew.

"That's a stirrup," he said.

"A what?"

"A stirrup. It's used to hold the feet when you want to examine the vagina or rectum. Here I'll show you." He got up on the table and put his feet in the stirrups. I almost died standing there looking at that beautiful ass. I could even see his dick through the white pants. "Spreads 'em wide open," he said. "Want to try?"

"No, no. Just curious," I said.

"Well, if you're curious let me show you," he said. "You gotta learn these things, and I'm just the dude to give you a live demonstration."

My heart was pounding so hard I knew he could hear it as he jumped off the table, undid his belt, pulled off his pants and jockey shorts, and stood with his back to me.

"A demonstration," he said as he bent over and pulled his cheeks apart. "You see, or rather you don't see the old asshole too good this way. It's okay for a quick finger rectal, but for a good look up the old canal . . ." he hopped up on the table, put his feet in the stirrups, spread his ass wide open, and explained "you use the stirrups."

My cock was rock hard instantly. There I stood with a Greek god naked before me, his ass spread open, his half-hard cock lying over to one side, and his heavy nuts hanging down almost to his asshole. I didn't know what to say. "Yeah, I see," I said.

"Want to feel? I'll teach you how to check a prostate. Put on one of those rubber gloves," he said.

I hesitated.

"Go ahead. You want to learn don't you?" he asked.

"Yeah," I said and put on the glove on my right hand.

"One's enough," he said. "Now squirt some of that K-Y on your finger tips."

I did as he said.

"Now come over here." I went over, and he pulled his cheeks apart with his hands. "Now stick your index finger up my ass slowly."

I can hardly remember all of this; I was in such a fog. I couldn't believe what was happening. I wondered if he was gay. He must be. Maybe not. I didn't care. I did care. I couldn't get my thoughts straight.

"Come on. I'll show you how to feel a prostate. Nothing wrong with that, is there?" he asked.

"No. I . . . I . . . Uh . . . I just . . . I don't know."

"Hey, don't worry. Are you shaky about poking your finger up another guy's ass?"

"Sort of, I guess."

"Nothing to worry about. It doesn't mean a thing. I'm just trying to show you how all this stuff works and what a prostate feels like. Come on now, get that finger in there." He laughed, grabbed my hand, and guided to it to his upturned ass.

I pointed my finger like making a phone call and slowly eased it into his puckered asshole.

"That's good," he said, "now ease it out and put two fingers in slowly."

I pulled my finger out and pushed the first two back in.

"Now your fingers are pointed the wrong way to feel my gland. Slowly turn your hand over, palm up, real slow."

I started turning my hand over and for the first time I noticed that his big dick was starting to harden.

"Good. Now you can feel the prostate with the tip of your fingers. Press up with your fingers."

I did.

"Feels sort of hard, huh?" he asked.

"Well, I guess," I said.

"I mean hard in comparison to the other side. Pull your hand in and out some, turn your fingers, and you'll feel how most of the inside is real soft, but the prostate is a lot firmer."

I turned my hand some and pulled back and forth a little. I did feel his prostate. Meanwhile, I had such a hard-on, I was sure he would notice. I could feel pre-cum oozing out of my dick. His cock was now rock hard and poking straight up in front of me. I was so excited, I didn't know what to do.

"Feel it?" he asked.

"Yeah," I said.

"I know you do. When you rub it like that, it gives me a hard-on. Hope that doesn't embarrass you. Ever seen another man's hard-on before?" he asked.

"Yeah," I blushed. "Sometimes."

"Circle jerks, I bet," he laughed.

"Yeah," I muttered.

"It's okay," he said, "just part of growing up. Got to learn how things work. Want me to show you on my cock?"

Before I could answer he had placed my bare left hand on his boner. I was shaking.

"No, no," he said, "you can't feel it with your palm. Use your fingers like this." He rubbed up and down on the huge erection with his finger tips. "See. Feel." I did it. "Yeah, that's right," he said. "Feel how hard the top is. That soft tube-like thing on the bottom is where your piss and cum come through."

I felt more pre-cum oozing out of my cock. I was in ecstasy. My fingers were still up his ass and my left hand was starting to actually jack him off. I was panting like a fool.

"Hey, you're excited," he said. "I can feel your pulse in my ass. I'm kind of excited, too. You rubbing my hard-on feels terrific. Grab it and jack it real good for a minute, will you?" he asked. "Keep feeling my prostate." In a few moments, he was breathing hard and said, "Well, all right, you're going to get me off. Feels good. Don't stop! Keep jacking me off."

I continued, getting faster and squeezing his beautiful cock harder.

"ALL RIGHT!" he said loudly and he started pumping his ass up and down with the rhythm. "ALL RIGHT. Fuck me with those fingers! Jack me off."

The "lesson" was forgotten, and now it was just pure sex. I couldn't stop; I couldn't think. I pumped faster and finger-fucked him harder.

"Good. Good," he almost yelled. "Fuck me good. Jack that cock. Jack it up and down. Squeeze it hard. Fuck me hard. Rub those fingers in me . . . faster . . . harder . . . faster."

My hand was moving so fast it was just a blur. "I'M THERE," he shouted. "I'M COMING. I'M COMING." His cock jumped rock hard, his prostate pulsed and five huge squirts of warm, starchy cum shot up across my arms, onto his stomach, and dripped down on my hand buried in his ass. Just as his last shot landed on my arm, I felt my own prick jump and a whole load of cum filled my jockey shorts.

"Oh shit," I said, "I came in my pants."

He laughed. "Look, ma, no hands. That's too bad you shot already," he said. "I wanted to get you off with the proctoscope."

"What?" I yelled.

"I was going to get your nuts off with the scope," he said. "It's fun. Hell, you can probably come again. Let's try it."

He got off the table, came over, and started unbuttoning my shirt. As he undid my belt, slipped my pants off, and pulled my sopping shorts off, he said "Hey, you got a good load. Let me clean you up some." He licked my dick and nibbled a gob of cum off my pubic hair. I couldn't believe any of this. I moved back.

"It's all right," he said. "Tastes good. I love cum. I love men and their bodies. You got a nice body. Nice nuts, too," he said. Then he nibbled at one of my balls.

Standing up, Jim instructed, "Okay. Demonstration number two coming up. Get up on the table, and put your feet in the stirrups."

I was scared but I did it. He strapped my ankles, then started to strap my chest down.

"Why this?" I asked.

"So you don't buck," he laughed.

He put on rubber gloves, squirted K-Y on his right hand and smeared a big gob on my asshole. He gently pushed one finger in. "Tight," he said. He then fucked the finger in and out a little. With his other hand, he started to jack me off like I had done him. "Relax. Loosen up some," he said. "Push down like you were taking a shit. That's it. Good. Getting looser. Now it's ready," he said. When he inserted the second finger, I jumped.

"Now, now. Don't tighten up. Just concentrate on relaxing. Just let me in real easy."

I relaxed.

"Good, good. Real good. You're nice and relaxed." He fucked in and out some. "You'll take the scope easily," he comforted.

He pulled out, got the scope from the cabinet, and smeared K-Y over the end.

"Now," he said, "you must relax and don't squeeze shut. This thing is only a little bigger than my two fingers and smaller than most cocks. Smaller than yours or mine, for sure," he laughed. "Ever had a cock up you?" he asked, and answered before I could, "No, no of course not."

"The secret is to relax, and let this iron dildo do its magic on you," he instructed. He rubbed my asshole, and I felt the cold tip of the proctoscope press against me. "Okay, now relax," he said, while he pushed the scope in.

I thought I was ripped open and screamed, managing to pull off the scope.

"Hey, hey, you're gonna hurt yourself. Relax, You're nervous. Here, let me give you a little pacifier." He kicked a step stool over to the head of the table, stood up on it, and presented his solid nine-inch cock to my face. "Suck this for a minute and relax," he said.

I felt like a baby, but that cock was irresistible. Taking the prick in my hands, I wrapped my lips around its mushroom head. Then I sucked, lapped, licked, and got such a fucking hard-on I wanted to jack myself off. When he saw my hand go to my own cock, he said, "No! That's for me. You just suck this. You must be ready now."

He took his position at the foot of the table and again pressed the scope into my ass. It hurt but not as much as before.

"Good," he uttered as he jacked my prick once or twice. "You're ready now. You're good and ready for this old reamer." He pushed it in further, and I had to pant to keep from tightening up. It was starting to feel a little good. He eased it up some more. It must have reached my prostate because he said, "Ooops, there goes the hard-on." He took my limp dick into his mouth and tongued me to a full erection again.

"Ah, good," he said, "now silver cock here will do the rest." He started fucking the chrome tube in and out, chanting "Fuck . . . fuck . . . fuck . . . fuck."

My ass was on fire, my cock was somewhere between hard and limp, and I wasn't sure if this felt good or not. As he continued, I knew I'd never get off with that fucking procto-scope, but I just relaxed and let him have my ass to do with what he liked. I wondered if his big dick was hard again. I wished I could suck it some more, instead of having this cold metal dong up my ass. He kept talking real sexy, playing with my nuts, fucking the dildo in me, but soon he also realized I wasn't going to cum.

"You're not going to make it with silver cock," he said. "I guess you want the real thing. Well, demonstration three is coming up. And I do mean up," he laughed.

He pulled the scope out of my ass, took off the rubber gloves, greased his rock-hard nine-incher with K-Y, and pulled the step stool around to the end of the table. He stood up on it, waved the big fuck pole at me, bent over, and aimed his beautiful man meat at my now ready hole. I met it with a thrust to get it nice and deep.

"Hey, you're one hell of a fuck," he said, ramming his hard fuckmeat all the way in. He pressed harder and harder, not pumping but just pushing. I could feel his big nuts mashed between our bodies. As he contracted his muscles, I could actually feel his deep boner throb in my ass. It was pure delight. I started pumping my ass, wanting more and more of that fuck-pole in me. I wanted to take in his nuts, feel his cock slip up my insides, and into my throat.

He responded with deep, slow thrusts that sent waves of joy into my guts. He fucked faster and faster, while my ass mas-saged that ivory tool from top to bottom. My own pulsed and throbbed in the air, but all I wanted was for him to come in me, to fill me with joy juice, to bathe my fucking ass with that mancream he had in his nuts, to leave that delightful dong in my ass until it softened and hardened again and again, and to fuck me forever.

He fucked and pumped and writhed and moaned, and as his big nuts bounced up for a shot of fuckcream, he took my cock into his mouth, letting my cock head get all the way down his throat. His cock burst, and I could feel quarts of fucksauce fill my happy ass. My cock responded with a quick spasm that sent my own joyjuice deep into his beautiful throat. It was wild. I have never felt anything like it, before or since.

—*St. Louis, Missouri*

160

Ron: "It Happened When I Was 16"

*I*t happened when I was sixteen. I was an only kid, living with my parents in the Colorado mountains where they ran a small ski resort. I was big for my age, and wanted to play football, so I spent about six months running five miles a day, lifting weights, and swimming. When the football season came along, my nagging mother wouldn't let me play, and my dad was too namby-pamby to do anything about it. I was really popular with the girls because I was the tallest, best-built kid in the school ("tall, dark and handsome," they said), but my mom wouldn't let me date, borrow the car, or have any contact with the chicks outside of school and on the school bus. At Thanksgiving time, since we hadn't had any snow, my father decided he would take my mom and me to Hawaii to avert a total blowup.

Our week in Hawaii was the pits. We stayed in the same room, with my mom nagging all the time because it had snowed back home, and our resort was closed. To top if off, we were on one of these little islands away from any action, and I was bored.

The day before we were scheduled to go back, I rented some snorkling gear and went with a chick to check out the fish and coral reefs, happy to possibly get in her suit. I was down about ten feet, about out of air, and ready to surface, when a large fish scared me. In trying to get away from him, my foot got lodged in some sharp coral. I panicked because of needing air, so I wrenched my foot free to get to the surface. In the process, I busted some foot bones, ripped open the skin, and pulled a groin muscle.

I woke up hours later with my mother, father, doctor, and male nurse standing around me, talking about what was needed to be done. The fracture was in a pretty touchy area of my left foot, and they had decided I shouldn't be moved from the island until some healing had started. Mother threw a fit, but the doctor was very firm.

The nurse said, "I've got an idea. The hospital is short of beds, and you're worried about the cost. I'm staying at a small hotel a block from here where Ron can get two meals a day, and I'll bring some food for the third meal. There's an empty room next to the bathroom, and it's real cheap." The doctor liked the idea, my mother wasn't sure, and I thought I'd really be bored stiff although the male nurse seemed to be a real nice guy.

My mother decided to think about it overnight. After the doctor departed, the nurse said we were real lucky because the doctor had just left a famous Boston hospital for the peace and quiet of Hawaii, and he was probably one of the best orthopedic surgeons around.

After my folks ran along, the nurse introduced himself as Dick. He admitted he was too young to be a nurse at twenty-two and was only an aide. Since I was still grubby from my afternoon salt-water experience, Dick proceeded to give me a bath. He washed my back, the backs of my legs, and scrubbed my ass, even washing in the crack and around my asshole. I was really shook when he wanted me to turn over, since I had gotten a roaring hard-on. He saw I was bugged, then saw what was bugging me and said, "Ah, Ron, don't sweat it. It's totally natural."

Continuing, he washed my chest, commenting that I was really well built. Then he washed my legs. When he got to my midsection, he handwashed my stiff cock and my balls, saying something about what a nice-sized cock I had and how he'd never touched an uncircumcised one before. By the time he finished, I was holding back cumming as hard as I could and was really glad it was over. Then he said that I had really dry skin, so he got out a bottle of Intensive Care lotion and began rubbing that into my chest. He did my neck, arms, legs, and again massaged my cock and balls. Somehow I kept from shooting, even after he had me roll over halfway to oil my back and asshole. Then he inserted a thermometer. Just as he did, I unloaded into the sheets with about three jerks.

Dick asked if he had hurt me with the thermometer.

"No, just a couple of spasms," I lied.

Dick then discovered what kind of spasms they were when he rolled me back and saw the mess on the sheets. "Hey, man, don't worry. It's natural. No big deal!" He pulled the new sheet up over me and left me to think and sleep. "I'm moving to the morning shift tomorrow, Ron, so I'll see you at seven," he said as he left.

The next morning, my mother agreed that it was a good idea for me to stay. So my dad paid for my room and board at the hotel for two weeks, gave me some extra money, made a deal with the doctor, and left with my mom for the airport.

Shortly, Dick brought me my breakfast and was in and out of the room until about three that afternoon when he helped me move to the hotel.

The place was more like a rooming house, but in a very

tropical setting. My room was upstairs with a little porch and a kind of thatched roof. His was at the other end of the hall, and the only bathroom was right next door to mine.

We had supper together that night, eating from bags he had gotten in a fast-food place nearby. Then he brought me his TV set, and we lay around all evening talking and watching the tube. Dick said that his girlfriend had split to model on the mainland for two months. When I asked what kind, he finally said that she had been a girlie magazine centerfold. When we talked some more, he told me he had also done a special feature with her for a national magazine. He decided I didn't believe him, so he went to his room and brought me back the issue featuring him with Karen, his girl. It made me really horny looking at those ten pages of nude pictures, and I noticed that I was paying some attention to Dick's pictures as well as to Karen's. They were both tanned all over and blond. Dick also had very curly hair, a real great build, and a good-sized, circumcised dick.

About nine that night, Dick decided it was time for my bath and massage. He started again on my back. First with soap and water, then with oils. Once more he did a real massage job on my asshole. I had never realized before that my asshole could be a turn-on. When Dick, after a time, turned me over, I again had a throbbing hard-on.

Because the hotel bed was lower than the hospital's, Dick sat alongside me. He was only wearing a towel. After the soaping and the rubdown, he placed my right arm down on his lap while he massaged my left. Soon he got to my cock, which he just kept on rubbing until I exploded all over his hand, my stomach and chest. While I was shooting, I felt his cock rise under the towel. I never thought to remove my hand.

The next night after Dick got home from work, he showered, wrapped himself in a towel, and propped me up on the porch to eat supper. Then we lay around on the bed watching TV and talking some more. As he started to give me my bath, he spilled some water on the floor and used the towel he had on to dry it up. He was naked when he sat beside me, and when he got through massaging my arms, he again laid my right hand in his lap right next to his cock. As he began working on my cock, his rose up right into my hand. I couldn't help but fondle it. He jacked me off to another explosion, and then lay beside me while I did the same to him.

After wiping up our messes, he talked about being horny because Karen was gone, and how curious he was about me. I admitted I was curious about him, too. He convinced me that what we were doing wasn't queer—we were just satisfying our curiosities.

I spent the next day reading some of the "girlie" magazines he had left for me, fantasizing about doing some other things with Dick. After he brought me supper that afternoon, he got me safely propped up in his old car and gave me an early evening tour of the island. He had a small bottle of wine, so we drank from the same bottle and probably appeared to anyone who saw us like a couple of drinking buddies. Dick patted my leg, we playfully punched each other, and as he was helping me out of the car when we got back to the hotel, we gave each other a big hug.

That night Dick helped me undress, then took off his own clothes. We lay side by side for a couple of hours watching TV and touching. I had an erection almost the whole time, and Dick brought up the subject of curiosities again.

"Can I try something on you, if I promise it won't hurt?" he asked.

"Sure!" I was tingling all over from wondering what would happen.

He got out the stuff to give me my bath again, washing both my front and back as usual. Then he lay down beside me and began licking my chest. He licked my nipples until they got hard and felt super. (I didn't know there was any feeling in a guy's nipples.) He licked my stomach, around my navel, and then began licking around my throbbing cock and balls. He licked my cock stem, pulled my foreskin back with his fingers, and then began to lick around the head. I had never before felt sensations like this in my life, and I thought I was going to faint at one point. Then he began going down on my cock, and I knew I couldn't hold back much longer. "Watch out, Dick. I'm coming," I said.

Dick went back to licking other places, and tongue-washed my thighs, the inside of my legs, and then, one by one, he licked and sucked my balls. He stopped for a minute and lay alongside me, hugging me to him. "God, that's a wild experience," he said.

"Boy, Dick, I almost let loose when you were sucking my cock, it felt so good."

He asked me if I had ever fantasized about sucking somebody. I said I had. He told me that he had been wondering what it would be like to suck somebody off and to have a dick in his ass.

Then he told me that he had never had a buddy like me and that I had a beautiful body and really turned him on. I admitted spending a couple of days jacking off while looking at his pictures with Karen in the magazine, and I had really wondered about the same things he was talking about.

"Ron...ah...can I suck you off and see what it's like to swallow your cum?"

We were hugging at the time, Dick alongside me with his erection pressed into my thigh. I just nodded my head, and he hugged me again. Then he began to lick my neck and chest and slowly worked his way down to my cock. The licking and sucking drove me wild for about a minute, causing me to shoot spurt after spurt of hot cum into his mouth. He swallowed it all, keeping my softening cock in his mouth for another couple of minutes.

We lay together for a little while so I could recuperate. Then I asked him if what he had just done had bothered him.

"No. You could use a little more salt, but otherwise it was just about what I had heard it would be."

I got up the nerve to begin licking his chest then and slowly worked my way down into the blond curls of his pubic hair. Finally, after doing everything I could remember he had done to me, I went as far down on his cock as I could, sucking and licking until he began to shudder and fill my mouth with shot after shot of hot sperm. I was amazed at myself for not gagging, but it wasn't a bad experience, and his clean man-smell really turned me on. We slept together that night—my first night in the same bed with anyone else in my whole life.

The next evening, after supper and my bath, Dick greased up my pole and fondled me until I couldn't take any more. He sat facing me with his legs straddling my stomach and slowly sat back on my hard cock. What a feeling! He had rubbed the head of my cock around his asshole, causing wild sensations that just about had me cumming a couple of times; but he was getting good at knowing when to stop and let me cool off. Finally he got my pole inched up into his asshole until his balls were lying on my stomach. I jacked him off while he rocked up and down on my throbbing member. Finally I filled his hot asshole with my fluids. Afterwards, we lay together, talking, fondling, and hugging. Before the night was over, we had each delivered to the other another mouthful of hot dessert.

The next night, after thinking about it all day, I asked Dick what having a cock up the ass felt like.

"Hurt a little at first, but after I got used to it it felt bitchin'."

I told him it was really wild having my cock in such a tight, hot hole, and he asked me if I wanted to put it in his ass again.

"Well, maybe . . . but what I was getting at was that I've been wondering how it would feel if you plugged me."

Dick massaged oil into my asshole for a long time, sliding in a finger, then two, and then three. I had already greased up his cock, so he lifted my legs up and slowly worked his circumcised eight-incher into my asshole. The pain really wasn't much — kind of like taking a big healthy crap. It was wild to feel the hot fluids fill me after he had pumped for a while, and I had an orgasm all over my stomach right after he had his.

Every afternoon for the next week, Dick and I sexed it up. Then when I went to the doctor for new x-rays, I discovered that Dick had fixed it so I could stay another week. (After all, they had had a terrible snowstorm back home, and I would have had a hell of a time getting along on crutches back there.) My mother bitched a lot on the phone when we told her, but finally agreed, sending another week's worth of money for the hotel and my food. Little did she know that my diet consisted of a lot of free, high protein cum.

From our long conversations, I am sure that all that we did was new for Dick, and it certainly was for me. It opened up a whole world, some of which I had never even dreamed existed before. Although I grew up and married a girl that turned out to be a lot like my mother, and although I had a couple of other physical relationships with girls, nothing ever matched the feelings, thrills, and excitement of those couple of weeks in Hawaii with Dick.

It's almost eleven years since that time, and I'm divorced and free. I spend a lot of time working with a scout troop, and there's a beautiful, tall, blond teenager that really seems to like me. In fact, he's from a broken home, and we're going camping next month.

Ron: Eleven Years Later

I'm a tall, dark, and handsome guy of twenty-seven who had his first sexual experience in Hawaii about eleven years ago. I hope you remember the story, because if you do this one will make a lot more sense. [See story above. — *Editor*] After my two weeks' worth of tremendous experience with a

bedded down for the night.

"Hey, Dave, I hate to bitch, but this sleeping bag isn't gonna keep me warm if it gets one degree colder," I said.

"Well, what my buddy and I do when it gets cold and we're out here is stick one bag inside the other. Then we both crawl into the same bag. They're double bags so they're big enough!"

I can't tell you for sure if I had any other motive than staying warm, but the idea appealed to me, so I told Dave we should do it if it was okay with him. It was obviously very okay. So I watched while his beautiful near-naked body put my sleeping bag inside of his. We then crawled in and lay side by side. I was warm as toast, and the touch of his skin felt really great.

Dave asked me a lot about myself, and we probably talked for two hours, instead of sleeping, At what seemed like an appropriate time, I told Dave that I was really impressed by him and that he was a lot of fun to be with. "I've never spent a lot of time around a teenager, Dave, and I didn't know how to act around that Scout troop. But you're more like a buddy near my own age than a kid."

He rolled toward me and gave me a little hug. I shifted my leg to respond, and it touched a very hard object in his shorts which I quickly noticed was no small thing. His hug was tentative, but it also felt like he'd been starved for someone to cling to. I hugged him back pretty hard. I could feel things beginning to come to life in my own shorts, so I had to back away a bit so he wouldn't find out, but once, a little later in our moonlight conversation, his leg bumped my obvious erection. I woke up a number of times that night to feel the very soft, firm warmth of his skin. It was totally unlike any feeling I had had in the last eleven years.

The next morning we lay around and chatted until the sun hit our sleeping bags, then we got up, pissed, and washed in the stream. It was really obvious that Dave was checking out my body every chance he got, and when I changed shorts his eyes didn't blink for fear he would miss something. After breakfast, we packed up and hiked around most of the day. We fished some, but caught nothing.

We spent the afternoon in the sun without shirts on and found a fairly warm little pond where we skinny-dipped. After supper, when the sun went down, it got cold pretty fast, and we decided to get in the sleeping bags to keep comfortable.

"Ya know, Ron, one thing I learned about camping that makes it easier is if you sleep without your shorts on you can wear 'em two days in a row, and the dirty ones won't stink up your pack."

"Fine with me," I said, and crawled into the cool bag naked. Dave went to take a leak, and I could see his beautiful profile with his large, swinging cock in the moonlight as he came back to crawl into the bag.

My mind flooded with the experiences of my sixteenth year as I lay beside the warm body of Dave. I had a roaring hard-on as Dave pressed into my side, his arm across my chest, and his head cradled in my arm.

"God, if I could have a dad, I wish it could have been a person like you," he said in a soft whisper.

I couldn't resist checking, so I moved my leg into the rock-hard flesh of his turgid cock. I asked him what he missed about a father, and he told me he never had anybody to have any "man talk" with, and he had a lot of questions with nobody to provide the answers. I knew we would be going back home the next day and wouldn't have another night in a sleeping bag together for a while, so, even though I was scared, I asked him what kind of questions he had.

"Oh, you know . . . same kind of stuff you probably went through when you were my age."

"Like?"

He looked me in the eye. "Like, you know . . . what it's like to be married . . . and about sex, and why I get hard-ons at the wrong times, and . . ."

I interrupted him. "You mean like right now against my leg?"

"Yeah!" His hand was across my chest.

"Dave, it happens to everyone. If you move your hand down a ways you'll discover that it even happens to old men like me."

He slid his hand slowly down my stomach and touched my cock. "Wow, it's hard," he whispered as he continued to feel it.

I panicked about the situation, knowing I was about to take it farther. "Well, kid, all of that is totally normal. If you're worried about getting an erection now with another guy in the same sack, it's because you're longing to touch him. Warm skin can make you horny."

He continued to feel my almost bursting cock, but I just didn't dare take a young virgin teenager beyond that point, so I didn't dare touch him back. He finally fell asleep with his hand still on my cock, and I stayed awake fighting my feelings for most of the night. By the time we started driving home the following afternoon, we had really become close friends. He drove my Porsche until the traffic got heavy, then talked a storm as I drove on to his house.

I got a big hug after we unloaded the stuff, and we decided on dinner two nights later. I fought with lots of my feelings that night, but finally decided what Dick the nurse had taught me about love and affection when I was Dave's age had become one of my best memories. I had wanted it. It appeared that Dave wanted it also, and I desperately wanted to share the experience with him.

Two weekends later, I got the use of a terrific condo at a place called La Mancha in Palm Springs. A heated pool and jacuzzi were in the very private, walled-in back yard. Palm Springs gets really hot during the summertime, but the evenings are fabulous, and the place was air conditioned. I had off from Friday afternoon until the following Wednesday morning. When I got the whole thing set up I asked Dave if he would like to go along. I met his mother, who seemed to like me. She thought I was a Scout leader who'd keep her kid out of trouble and away from the house so she could do her thing. In other words, she quickly said yes to the idea. We packed and went down I-10 to spend four days together.

The sun was just going over the mountains when we arrived, and we immediately hit the private pool in our birthday suits. Dave was excited, and we goofed around in the pool, hugging and talking for an hour or two. I got him dressed in some Palm Springs–type shorts and a half T-shirt that I'd bought in Hollywood. Dave looked spectacular, and we went downtown to have dinner and mingle with the natives. For Friday night, there was a pretty good crowd, and my teen friend attracted a lot of admirers before we decided to go back to the condo. Dave hit the pool again for a night swim. Since we'd turned the water heater up, the pool temperature was in the nineties. Dave was obviously horny and missed no opportunity to bump against me. He even swam underwater between my legs, brushing my half-soft cock a couple of times. He soon got me very horny, too.

I sat neck-deep in the water on the pool steps, and Dave came to sit next to me. I pulled him onto my lap, and we snuggled together, softly rubbing our hands over each other.

"If I'm guessing right, Dave, I think you'd like for us to play with each other. Right?"

I felt a little bold, but he'd really gotten me worked up, and my hard cock was pressed against his leg.

"God, yes Ron. I've been dreaming about touching you all over and playing with you . . . and you playing with me."

I was rubbing his shoulders and chest with one hand and his back with my other. I switched to his lower back and lower stomach, coming immediately into contact with his eight-inch circumcised tool. Soon we were rubbing and fondling each other all over, lying together in the water with his face next to mine. He chewed on my ear a bit, and then kissed me on the cheek and lips. His hands explored my cock and balls. Slowly we jacked each other off, hands going everywhere, even fingering each other's assholes. His cock was a bit longer than mine but not as thick. In short order we both creamed in the water, and Dave's orgasm was accompanied by lots of heavy breathing, some moans, groans, and heavy hugging.

We slept together in the master bedroom in one big, rolled-up ball, and Dave couldn't seem to get enough hugging and touching. We made our own meals the next day and didn't put on any clothes until after the sun went down. Playing, fondling, and kissing filled most of the day, along with sunning, and massaging each other all over with baby oil. Around noon, we ended up inside the condo on the big living-room sectional, and I decided it was time Dave found out how much better a mouth felt than a hand on his cock. He exploded very quickly and recovered in only a couple of minutes, filled with curiosity about what it would be like to suck me. My cock was a mouthful, but he was slow, tender, and gentle, and quickly learned to take most of it until I felt my cock-tip touch the back of his throat. After my explosion, which he swallowed without much trouble, we talked about it, fondled each other, and ended our lunch hour by getting a dessert from each other in a side-by-side sixty-nine.

The next few days were an absolute dream. The big, handsome, blond teenager was totally turned on about trying anything and everything with me. We both had orgasms about four times each day—cumming in each other's hands, mouths, and asses. We had both given each other tongue baths from top to bottom, and I do mean bottom. Rimming Dave's asshole was really exciting for both of us (something I'd never tried before), and he did a terrific job of doing the same to me before finally putting his long tool into my spit-lubricated ass. After trying everything else, I think Dave's favorite pastime became sucking my cock. He seemed to enjoy that more than receiving a sucking. He especially enjoyed licking around my foreskin.

Dave still comes over a lot, and we camp out, go to the beach, or to the Springs quite regularly. I'm engaged to be married again after two years of bachelorhood, and Dave has a very steady flame, but we enjoy our deep, caring male relationship and plan to continue our physical experiments after we get married. By the way, both of our girlfriends think he's my cousin and that I'm committed to be responsible for him. I am.

—*Reno, Nevada*

At Sea With Twelve Hundred Sailors

M y story goes back to 1946 when I was in the U.S. Navy on board a heavy cruiser. I boarded the ship at San Pedro, CA., straight from boot camp at Sampson, N.Y. We were on our way to Japan—as the U.S. Occupation Forces—following World War II.

On the ship, there were mostly seasoned sailors, who had served during the war, and planknowners, a term given to those who served on the ship since it was commissioned. We who came from boot camp were called "swabbies," "skinheads," and some other uncouth names. Swabbies got all the shit details and abuse from the ship regulars, but we accepted this as unwritten Navy law.

One afternoon, Johnny (another swabbie) and I were on a cleaning detail, washing down the decks below where we bunked. In the far corner of the compartments where the laundry bin was located, four or five guys were sitting and lying about on top of the laundry bin and nearby sacks. Four of the guys were seasoned sailors; the other one, Bob, came aboard with us and had somehow or other wormed his way into their favor (probably giving them blow-jobs). We slowly worked our way over to where they were, and I could see they were eyeing us all the way.

As we approached them, one of the guys, in a prone position rubbing his crotch, yelled out "Hey swabbies, how about sucking some nice juicy cock."

A second guy remarked, "Aw shit! Let's grab them and fuck them in the ass. I ain't got laid since we left San Pedro."

Well, we both got nervous. Being eighteen and naïve as hell, I had no idea that they meant it. Johnny and I were two skinny guys, me short and he tall, and certainly no match for these five fuckers. Looking at their crotches, I could see erections bursting in their pants. They were looking at us as if we were two 42nd Street tarts. I opened my mouth, saying, "Ain't nobody gonna fuck me, unless I want them to."

They naturally laughed, and before we knew it, the four of them jumped up, grabbed us, and pulled off our dungarees. Bob, the swabbie, pulled my face between his legs and was trying to shove his hard cock into my mouth. It was hot below decks, and I could smell the musky aroma of his crotch in my nostrils. He said if I bit him he'd bash my fuckin' head in. The other guy Joe mounted me and was trying like hell to shove his stiff cock up my virgin ass. I held my ass real tight, which made him mad as hell. He cussed me and kept slapping my thighs, repeating "Loosen up goddamit."

I would not. He then shoved his dry finger way up my ass with such force that he must have bruised it inside. He kept rotating his probing finger in my ass, trying to relax it. I got so tired of keeping my ass tense, and his probing finger was hurting me something awful, that I relaxed it. He then remounted me again, clasping his arms around me, cupping both his hands on my tits, squeezing them roughly, while grunting and thrusting with such force that I felt his hard cock tear through my ass with such pain that I let out a scream. My yell was muffled by Bob, who then shoved his dripping cock to the back of my throat, making me gag. He held it there, pulling my head towards his crotch and humping my mouth as if it was a cunt. Soon my mouth was full of red pubic hair and sweet tasting pre-cum. I couldn't breathe as his pubic hair was smothering me. He kept my head pressed close to his crotch to prevent his cock from slipping out. This bird wanted badly to unload in my mouth and wasn't taking any chances of misfiring. His balls were all triggered up tightly and resting on my chin, so I knew the fuck was soon to inaugurate my mouth with his champagne. My jaw ached, and I was weary. I should have bit his cock off, but I was afraid I would hurt him (or he would hurt me), so I spared him. Anyway, he may need the fucking thing someday. No sense leaving notches on it.

Meanwhile, the bronco-buster on top of me was fucking me like there was no tomorrow, diggin' his nails into my tits. God, was he hot. I must have been a good lay, since my ass was burning with pain. The more I struggled, the deeper and faster his thrusts became. I only wished I was enjoying it as much as he was. He sure was working his fucking ass off. I could feel his chest, wet with perspiration, soaking my back and his stubbly unshaved beard rubbing against my shoulders. He had me gripped so tightly, I couldn't move. I was completely locked in.

Bob was still fucking me in my mouth, and my neck was aching because I was in an awkward position. He kept repeating, "Suck it, you bastard, and lick my balls, too."

He said that to impress the guys with how macho he could be. Joe blurted out between grunts "Hey Bob, what a nice tight ass he has. You ought to try him when I'm through with him. I'll have his ass nice and lubricated wtih my cream."

"Okay!" Bob replied. "Great! I want some of that ass too!"

I gulped when I heard that. Bob said, "I'm gonna unload any

minute now, and he better not spit any of it out."

Well, he came first, and it seemed as if it was a gallon. I couldn't swallow it all, and it dripped down over my chin and onto his red hairy balls. As I recall, it was sweet tasting and not unpleasant. It tingled my throat a little, and he insisted I lick it clean or he'd beat the shit out of me. Well, what the hell! The act was already done. What did I have to lose? I was tired of it all, so I licked him clean, and oh, how he sighed.

Needless to say, I could sense my ass-loving friend, Joe, was about to climax. I could feel his cock throbbing and swelling inside me. Boy, did he come full force. His hot cum spurted up my ass, and he thrust deeply with each spurt. The warm jism was burning inside of me, yet the emulsive nature of the cum was soothing after a few minutes, especially when it coated the battered area. Boy, was my ass battered! It seemed the cum would never stop. It was like taking a fuckin' enema. Boy, were these guys loaded! I was completely exhausted.

My friend, Johnny, meanwhile, was being fucked by the other guys. One of the guys was fucking him hard and fast and really sailing into him. He would now and then say, "Come on, you guys. You're hurting me."

I could vouch for that. He, however, seemed to enjoy sucking their cocks, and did they have large ones. The two guys who had stolen my maidenhood decided to reverse positions. Their cocks were hard again after resting for a few minutes and keeping me pinned down all the while. I needed the rest, too, since I had come also and felt sticky on my belly area. When they decided to make the move, in that split second I jumped free, breaking away from them. I grabbed the wet mop nearby, speared it in their direction, and ran like hell with a burning painful ass to my compartment to lick my wounds. They did not pursue me, but I heard one say, "We'll get him next time."

My friend, Johnny, was still there, and he didn't resist. As a matter of fact he was fucked by three of the guys and blew their cocks, too. Those guys had a ball. I touched my asshole and found a little blood on my finger; I knew I wasn't having my period either. I was furious. My ass was sore for two days, and so was poor Johnny's ass, but we did not report it. Things like this happen quite often, especially with twelve hundred guys aboard in close quarters. Out at sea for months, a little screwing and blowing goes on in all corners, lockers and cabins.

One night when I got off midwatch (12 midnight to 4 a.m.) guard duty, I decided to revenge myself on the guy (Joe) that fucked me. I carefully approached his bunk with a handful of cum (mine) which I had carefully cupped in my hand. I then smeared his sleeping face with it. He awoke dumbfounded, mumbling incoherently. I said, "Next time I'll put it in your mouth," and walked away laughing.

The following day, he wanted to kick my ass in, but when I told him what a poor sport he was, he backed away, smiled and said "Friends," extending his hand to me. I said, "Okay, why not, after all you busted my cherry," which gave him a laugh.

It was soon all forgotten since we worked, slept and ate together. But every now and then he would squeeze my ass or cup my crotch. He was dying to get into me again. Quite a few times he'd jump into the sack with me, when I was lying there reading a magazine or writing a letter or something. He'd start pinching my tits and fingering my crotch and ass. After a while I just let him do it as it kept him quiet, but sometimes I thought, *What Joe really wanted was for me to fuck him.* I never suggested it, even though I would have loved to give him a dose of what he gave me.

Strangely enough, we became good buddies from then on. Joe was horny and any ass staring in his direction was not safe. He was a chancy guy, but I really got to like him later on. I would always tell him that I wanted my virginity back. He would in turn grab his crotch and aim it at me in a joking gesture.

One thing always puzzles me. In the all-male porn films, cocks glide in and out of asses as if they were on roller skates — as if fucking was frictionless. That is not true. There *is* friction there!

—*Brooklyn, New York*

"Mr. Greene, when did you first suspect your passion for golden showers was getting out of hand?"

Hawaiian Lays

C all me John. I'm a fairly well-known tennis pro in some circles, twenty-eight, and married for two years with a one-year-old son and one well on the way. I was wrapping up a four-week tennis stint in Hawaii, staying at the Kuilima Hyatt on the North shore of Oahu. I had been very lonely and was trying to stay away from some of the hot-blooded and very available women I had been instructing, many of whom obviously wanted to climb my muscular six-foot-one frame, run their hands through my naturally curly blond locks, and play with my eight-inch club (I heard two of them discussing me once, and one called me a "gorgeous stud god." Not bad, huh?)

One night I had driven down to a town called Haleiwa, about twelve miles from the hotel and past the famous surf at Sunset Beach. I'd had a couple of beers, a hamburger, and some greasy fries, and passed some time playing video games. Nursing a big case of the "lonelies," I decided to go back to the hotel, take a late night dip down the beach, and knock off early.

My headlights showed a kid running beside the road in the same direction I was driving. I slowed a bit, and as I neared, he swung around and stuck out his thumb. He looked like a clean-cut local kid, so I stopped and picked him up. He was breathing really hard, sweaty, excited, and wearing only a pair of surfer shorts. He spoke a pidgin slanguage, but was easy to understand. "How far you going?" I asked.

I glanced at his young, beautiful face as headlights from oncoming cars lit up his details. He'd obviously been crying. He looked straight ahead. "I dunno, man . . . as far as you're goin' . . . then I'll catch another ride."

He wiped an eye with the back of his hand. He was probably part Hawaiian, I thought . . . dark-skinned, lean, muscular, and very shook up. "I'm staying at the Kuilima . . . I can get you that far."

"Thanks, man. Thanks for pickin' me up . . . I really needed to get outta there."

Slowly, I got him to tell me what had happened. Two Samoan guys from his school had gotten drunk and found him walking alone. They'd tried (at least) to rape him as near as I could tell. "You think you're hurt? . . . ah . . . "

"Kimo," he offered. "Ah, I don't know, man . . . "

"John," I said.

"I, ah . . . I'm not sure, sir."

His breathing was slowing, and he started looking toward me when he talked. "Look, Kimo . . . can I take you to your home or something . . . maybe a doctor?"

"Oh, no!" he quickly answered. "My mother's split with her boyfriend until . . . ah, besides, that's where those guys got me . . . I couldn't go there."

"How 'bout a doctor?"

"Naw, sir . . . I'll be OK. They cost money, and besides, I'd be scared."

When I got to the turnoff to the hotel, I didn't take it and just kept on driving.

"Oh, sir, don't worry. I'll be OK."

Slowly, I began to develop a plan, and I don't know what caused me to want to get involved with this native kid, but I did. "Look, let's do this. We'll go to my hotel . . . maybe best if you come in on the ocean side and not through the lobby the way you're dressed. You come up to my room, take a shower, clean up, we'll check to be sure you're OK, get you some food, and go from there."

He hesitated, then agreed after some discussion. He thanked me for helping him as we got out of the car in the parking lot. I gave him the room number, patted his back, and we took off in separate directions.

I saw him much better in the room with the lights on. He was a beautiful surfer kid, and he looked quite young. He smiled a "thank you," and said he'd be gald to leave right after he showered and not bother me. I quickly realized I very much did not want him to go. Putting a hand on each shoulder, I looked him in the eyes. "Kimo . . . I'm a pro athlete, and I've been around trainers for about ten years. I can check to see if you're damaged or not, get you some food, you can sleep here since you can't go home, and we'll figure something out in the morning."

He protested weakly, but I led him into the bathroom and began running the shower. He slipped off his trunks, and I stared a bit at his beautiful, uncircumcised cock, swaying from a patch of very black hair. As he showered, I pulled off my shirt, slipped on a clean pair of tennis shorts, and got out some baby oil and alcohol. Kimo came out into the suite wrapped in his towel, and I suggested he let me check him for damage from his attack. Without questioning he dropped the towel, lay down on the bed on his back, and raised his legs. I would have suggested he just bend over, but this position was obviously very suitable for what I had to do.

I rubbed some baby oil on my hands and lightly began to probe his asshole, asking him if it felt painful anywhere. He kept saying it felt funny and different, but not at all painful. I found no problems, but still continued probing and asking, noticing that his cock was quickly becoming erect. I got bold enough to insert the finger a little deeper and then to insert a second finger, but no pain was found anywhere.

"Just exactly what did they do, Kimo?"

"Well, the bigger guy got me down and got my shorts off, and then the other guy got on me an' started shovin' his cock at my hole. I'm yellin' for 'em to get off, so they get a knife outta the kitchen an' hold it to my balls . . . an' then I'm yellin' harder, and they start pullin' the skin on my dick and sayin' they're gonna cut the skin off . . . an' . . . an' they laid the knife on pretty hard, but it was dull an' I don't think nothin' happened."

Tears were again welling in his eyes as he remembered the experience.

"How'd you get away?"

"Well . . . the one guy is startin' to push further into me and pumpin', an' the other guys'll do anything when they're drunk. So somebody outside starts yellin' to shut up and beatin' on the door, an' they get scared . . . an' the one humpin' me wants to finish 'cause he says he's gettin' close, so they decide to take me out back. Well . . . when they're tryin' to move me, I kick the smaller guy in the balls, grab my shorts, an' run."

All the time he's telling the story, I'm massaging his asshole and he's got a throbbing erection.

"I don't see any cut marks, Kimo!"

He ran his hand over his throbbing cock holding it up for inspection. "You sure?"

I couldn't stop myself if I had to. In my best doctor fashion, I examined every inch of his beautiful seven-incher and his nice, round, hairless globes.

"Why did it feel so awful when they were touchin' me, and so good when you do it?" He seemed to be totally sincere.

I swallowed hard. This was all new to me. "Everybody loves to be touched lightly and easily. Nobody likes someone to get rough and touch without asking for it."

The spell was broken by a phone call from one of my horny women admirers, but I lied, saying I was calling home and then going to bed. Kimo hadn't eaten, so I called room service, and the kid stayed in the bathroom when it was delivered. I told Kimo to start eating while I took a shower, and since I noticed he was eating without anything on, I came out naked to get my snack. Kimo didn't try to hide his interest in my body.

"You're very great looking, John. You have a very big cock. I'll bet it's really big hard, huh?"

The kid seemed guileless, questioning everything, and getting me to admit that I was lonesome and really wanted to have his company. He made me show him a picture of my wife and kid, and then told me I was very lucky . . . that he'd never have the chance to have a "pretty lady" like her.

I got up from the table to lounge on the bed as he talked, and Kimo came over and sat beside me. "Can I check you out like you checked me?"

I laughed, nervously. "Hell, Kimo . . . nobody raped me tonight!"

"I know, but I'm curious, and I won't hurt you."

He got the baby oil, spread my legs, and began fondling my asshole, my balls, and my instantly erect cock. His touch was unlike anything I had ever felt before, and I almost stopped breathing for the wild sensations. He stopped his fondling, slid up beside me, and gave me a big hug. I hugged him back, and we were pressed together, cock to cock, for a long moment.

With a glint in his eye, he looked at me, and getting up on one elbow, said, "I got an idea I'd like to try, an' it won't hurt, so can I?"

I tried to get him to tell me, and finally agreed that I wouldn't get mad at him if it didn't hurt. He got up, walked around the bed, climbed on it and kissed my cheek. Then he nuzzled my ear and began licking my nipples and the hair on my chest. Soon his lips were on my stomach licking my navel, and his cock was conveniently within close reach. I began to fondle him as he began to nibble my cockhead, around the stem, and my balls. His fingers found my asshole, and mine again found his. He had positioned himself in such a way that his cock was within a few inches of my face, and I was slowly drawn to it like a magnet.

All of the longings I had suppressed while becoming a macho athlete began to come out. Soon I had his lean torso straddling my face and I was fondling his ass, finger fucking him, while licking his balls and sucking his cock. His mouth was doing miraculous (and very expert) things to my cock and balls, and a great explosion was beginning to build. He began sucking me harder, and I reciprocated as well as a novice could do (which he said later was pretty damn good). Soon I saw his balls, which were right above my eyes, begin to contract. I knew from my medical studies that he was about to do what I was going to do. I stopped sucking and warned him that I was coming. He moved his cock away from my face but continued to suck as I stroked him. I came in his mouth, which was obviously what he wanted, and he shot all over my chest. He drained me dry, sucking every drop from me, and then we showered together . . . the best shower I had ever had.

We slept more tightly wrapped up in each other than I had ever slept with Margie, and awoke the next morning to an hour of hugging, sucking, and fondling. Kimo told me that he'd had a few experiences with an older boy about a year before, and I told him that his friend had been a hell of a teacher. He was so smooth-skinned and hot, and so excited about my blond curly body hair and big cock . . . we seemed perfectly matched. I didn't answer my phone calls that morning. We showered together. I shaved, and then we went back to bed.

*　　*　　*

My frisky colt sat playfully on my stomach as if he were going to pin me. Instead he leaned over and kissed my lips, smiled, reached behind himself to fondle me to a full erection, and then asked me another question, "Hey, John . . . you know last night when I wanted to try something and you said OK if it didn't hurt?"

"Yeah."

"Well, it worked out OK, right?"

"Oh, God, Kimo . . . very OK!"

"So I'm curious about 'nother thing, an' I don't think it'll hurt ya, so can I try?"

He had oiled up my cock and was sitting on my stomach, so it was obvious what he had in mind and I couldn't imagine trying to stop him.

I fondled his asshole as he played with my cock, and slowly he began pushing himself back down on it. I felt my turgid cock slide slowly into his hot tunnel just past the head, and it was incredibly tight, hot, and sexy. Soon I was all the way into his chamber, and he slowly began to motion up and down as I fondled his beautiful organ. I didn't want the tremendous feelings to stop, but soon I filled his hot ass with a load of my cum. He looked ecstatic with the feelings my spurting cock was giving him inside.

We lay and played, talked, fondled, and sucked for hours. I got in a couple of lessons that afternoon while Kimo went out on the beach. Then, that evening, we tried it all over again.

I had even found a motherly lady working at the hotel, who lived nearby, who could keep Kimo for a few months until school was out. Between playtimes we discussed that and got him to agree it was a good deal. That night, after asking lots of questions about the feelings, Kimo promised to be very careful and started massaging my well-lubricated asshole for a while. I got him positioned over my up-raised ass and felt him slide past the moment of pain into the inner world of pleasure. In my twenth-eighth year I finally really got "laid." Oh, what a feeling!

PART TWO

*I*t's a year and a half since my encounter with Kimo, and to say it was revolutionary to my life would be the understatement of the year. When we had to part, amid much tears and promises to write, call, and keep in touch, I had some guilt feelings over what we had done together. I quickly had to forget them because on the day I got home, my wife, Margie, had a miscarriage. Because of the complications, the doctors cut her tubes and said she couldn't have kids. Shortly, I got a big offer to be Pro in a brand new facility in another city, so we moved. While Margie was getting over the trauma of her crisis, she was also becoming much more loving and horny with me . . . a bigger turn-on for her than for me at that time.

We started having oral experiences for the first time since we met, and I found myself imagining Kimo—which made our little marriage experiences much better for me. I had told Margie of the sharp, homeless Hawaiian kid I had met, and everything about our meeting except for the sexual. (I said that two guys had beat him up, and I'd taken him to the hotel to fix his wounds.) She was very interested in Kimo and talked to him when he started calling every other Sunday night (collect). She suggested to him once that he come for the summer when school was out, since we had more space in our new home. I was terrified about what might happen if he came, and excited at the prospect all at the same time.

I started giving tennis lessons to the eighteen-year-old son of the cook lady in the Pro Shop restaurant. He reminded me a little of Kimo, since he was a dark-skinned, very handsome Mexican kid who wore tennis shorts a little too tight, and dressed and talked very sexually. Billy intrigued me a lot, and one night, after his lesson, I found myself accepting his offer of a Jacuzzi together.

We fondled each other for a long time, and the water was a little milk-colored when we finished. Billy was very forward in his desire to use my body, and I was doing a poor job of controlling myself from attacking his moist, dark, muscular five-foot six-inch frame, or his great, thick, five-and-a-half-inch cock. He was a perfectly proportioned creature with a lot more male-male experience than I had, and I was very fearful of what would happen if I stayed close to him for too long.

Margie, meanwhile, seemed horny all the time, and I often found her lying naked with our little boy, fondling and being fondled. We even started being nude at home all the time, and one of Margie's new girlfriends started giving her *Playboy, Playgirl, Variations, Forum* and a booklet on lesbianism loaded with pictures (which she read often, it seemed). One day she brought home a copy of a male magazine called *In Touch* and a little *Readers Digest*–sized booklet called *First Hand.*

She devoured the contents of everything she found, and got me to read whatever she brought home. We talked a lot about being "open" and having an "open" marriage, having other couples over who might be "free" or a girlfriend or two. She always would bring up Kimo, and the idea of having him come for the summer, and she asked me hundreds of questions about how he looked—like he was some kind of fantasy to her.

Kimo arrived in June and it seemed more exciting for Margie than for me. Oh, I loved him and wanted to be with him, but we had to be very careful around her and that wasn't easy. He'd grown a bit, and someone who knew how to make a Hawaiian kid look like a knockout had styled his long hair. He was even more spectacular than I had remembered him, and Margie was really impressed.

Less than a day passed before we all began to be nude together. Kimo loved to lie on the couch cuddling and fondling the baby, and Margie encouraged the baby to play with Kimo's cock. (It was the best way she knew of at the time to see what it looked like hard.) John Junior was also interested in the experience, and I was very frustrated. The third night that Kimo was with us, after watching some TV in the nude, Margie grabbed both of us by the hand and said, "Cummon, you guys . . . it's bed time."

When we got to the bedroom, she threw back the covers and had Kimo lie down on his back in the middle, indicating that I should get on one side of Kimo while she got on the other. "OK, you guys . . . I've been reading these *Variations* magazines, and I've got an idea. You see . . . we work two on one and make everybody feel good. First, you and I will work on Kimo . . . then we'll do you, and then you guys will have me all worked up and you can work me over."

Margie acted like the Program Director. We were to tongue-wash Kimo from the neck down. When I got part way and began to hesitate, she scolded me. "Cummon, Johnny . . . you read the same stuff I read, and we both say this stuff is OK . . . then you act like it ain't. Kimo obviously is enjoying it. Cummon, Johnny, get into it!"

We all let go. Margie and I sucked Kimo's cock together, or she'd suck his nuts while I worked his cock over. We'd switch, all the while Kimo was fondling us and we were fondling each other. We all came at least twice in our three-hour orgy and ended up sleeping together. In fact, Kimo never slept in the guest bedroom after that.

The next night we tried a number of other things, including Kimo inserting in Margie with me licking his balls and her outer lips. Kimo then took me in the ass while Margie sucked him off, and Margie took Kimo up her ass with me in her cunt, etc. It almost seemed that her favorite thing was to watch Kimo and me sucking and fucking each other. Once in a while she would get a hand into the act or lick something, but most of the time she really got excited about how we played and looked to-gether.

Later that week, Margie's mother went to the hospital for something pretty routine, but Margie still had to fly out to be with her for a few days. You can't imagine how brokenhearted I was that she had to leave Kimo alone with me, but I decided to be brave.

Our first night together was a four-hour repeat of everything we had ever done in our get-acquainted sessions in Hawaii. Kimo and I must have had at least three explosions apiece that night. Then Billy met Kimo the next day on the tennis court, and that opened the door to my first (and hopefully not last) two-day orgy with two other beautiful young males. Billy loved to do everything, and Kimo and I were both learning as fast as we could. Billy and Kimo invented some three-way daisy chain methods of getting everyone serviced at once (not new inven-tions for others, just for us).

About two hours before I was due to leave to pick up Margie at the airport, Billy arrived and we decided to have one more romp. Billy turned on the cassette deck, and put on a hell-of-a-strip performance with Michael Jackson (recorded, of course). Then Kimo got in the act and turned out to be a terrific natural

184

LA-2001-1-1279

dancer. Soon the three of us were intertwined in a wild session that had me lying on my back, looking up at two dark cocks an inch from my nose, one long and skin covered, one stubbier and skinless. The male odors were clean and very erotic to me, and my fingers did the walking into their ass-cracks as I licked them both. I attempted to suck two at once, while somebody's mouth was working magic on my cock and another was licking my balls. As the cassette ended, we broke to turn it off, and someone started applauding.

Margie had taken an earlier flight and had been able to watch most of our show. I was embarrassed, and the two boys were acting awkward, but she put us at ease quickly by telling us she was glad we were practicing for her return. Before Billy went home, Margie invited him for dinner the following night. "Don't bother to dress up, Billy. You won't need clothes for long."

Tomorrow night could prove interesting, but then that's chapter three.

—Los Angeles, California

"Shortest vampire I've ever seen!"

185

"I Stroked His Beautiful Black Shaft"

While I was a senior at our local university, I worked as a sales clerk on the graveyard shift at a neighborhood grocery store. Almost every night during my shift, there would be a dead period between 2 a.m. and 5 a.m. I normally passed away these hours by restocking the shelves or by taking inventories. But one evening, while I was crouched on the floor in between two gondolas of canned goods, a middle-aged black man entered the store. He'd just moved into one of the nearby apartment buildings. I presented him with my expected businesslike courtesy. He became a semi-regular customer on my shift, dropping by on his way home from work at one of the local factories.

One evening while I was very bored, I pulled up an empty milk crate and browsed through some of the magazines on display behind the counter. While I was reading one particular article, my black friend entered the store for some cigarettes. He was very hot and sweaty after a busy shift at the factory. He peeled off his tank top, and his smooth ebony chest glistened with sweat. He massaged his shoulders as I turned to ring up his purchase. Then he quickly grabbed the magazine that I'd left open to an article on masturbation. He chuckled very softly and began to confide in me that masturbation was usually the way he spent most of his evenings. While he began to detail his favorite jack-off fantasy, he very slowly groped his own crotch. I couldn't help but notice the enormous bulge beginning to build between his legs. My mouth began to drool.

When he had finished describing his fantasy, he smiled at me with his sensuous green eyes and said, "Would you like to suck me?" My heart climbed into my throat as I tried to remind him that I had three hours left on my shift. He just grinned and said, "Turn on the door buzzer, and we'll step into the back room." By now the bulge in his dirty blue jeans had inched half-way down his left leg, and I could barely resist the urge to drop to my knees right there. The fear of being discovered by the owner turned irrelevant as we approached the back room. All I wanted was to wrap my lips around that amazing black rod of his.

He unbuttoned his pants and slipped them down to his

ankles. Then I quickly peeled off his blue, mesh bikini briefs, discovering the treasure I'd been craving.

As I began to lovingly stroke his beautiful black shaft, I took each of his balls into my mouth and swished them around inside as I savored their sensuous taste. When I looked up to his cock, it had climbed to its full potential—a raging twelve inches of delicious man meat. I knew I wouldn't be able to get the entire length of his tool into my mouth but I was determined to give it a hell of a try. I vigorously licked up and down the full length of his throbbing shaft as I massaged his gorgeous buns with my right hand, twitching his nipples with my left. He moaned and whispered as I worked steadiy on each inch of his pulsating cock. Suddenly alarms shot off in my head, ears, and heart as the door buzzer rang. I deftly gathered my composure and entered the store to find a pair of young girls searching for the best buy in frozen pizzas. I nervously assisted them in selecting four large pizzas, rang up the purchase, sacked their merchandise, and courteously escorted them to the door.

When I re-entered the stockroom, I found my black friend slowly and sensuously stroking his male genitalia. I gathered his manhood into both of my hands and began to fondle his cock and balls lovingly, apologizing for the interruption. He smiled and leaned over to kiss me. As his lips enveloped mine, I was filled with an overwhelming warm feeling that made my own erection grow more intense. While I was caressing his broad and muscular shoulders and nibbling on his neck, he asked, "Do you have any Vaseline?" I darted out again into the store and returned with a small bottle that I'd just stocked the other night. He smiled and began removing my pants. When he slipped my jockey shorts down to my knees, his mouth expertly traveled down my stomach and around my navel. I was beginning to feel quite weak.

By now, I was willing to give in to any of his fantasies; I was all his. As he sucked my cock into his warm, wet mouth, he thoroughly applied half of the Vaseline to my awaiting anus and the other half to his throbbing manhood. When he had finished with the preparations, he replaced his mouth with his warm velvety-soft hand and began to pump at a rather steady and vigorous pace. Within minutes I was arching my back and shooting my entire load onto his face. He stood, engulfing me within his massive arms while I licked every ounce of cum from his beautiful black face. He once more rewarded me with a long and loving deep kiss.

Then I slowly turned and positioned myself on top of some boxes as he began to massage my buttocks. Slowly and gently he entered my nervous and anxiously awaiting love-hole. When all twelve inches of his rock-hard meat was pulsating within my body, he once more pu; his massive arms around me for a compassionate bear hug and whispered, "I don't want to hurt you. I just need you so much. Have you ever been fucked before?" I sheepishly confessed that I had.

He kissed me on the back of the neck and began his long penetrating strokes in and out. After he was sure that I could take his entire rod, he expertly began to pick up the pace of his strokes. My thighs, hips, and stomach muscles were all quivering with the constant and massive movement within my lower body. I groaned softly as his cock entered deeper and deeper with each successive stroke. Moments before he reached orgasm, he enveloped me once again with his warm and enormous body. His sweat-drenched upper torso rested on my back as his hips pistoned in and out of my hot, wet buttocks.

He moaned only for a second as he shot load after load of hot cum into the deepest recesses of my bowels. After the last jet of love juice left his body and was deposited within mine, he sighed a long and relaxed breath of air. We remained motionless for a few minutes before either of us began to regain our composure.

When we returned to the store, he thanked me, caressed my buttocks, and strolled out the door. I've never told anyone about this before, but that was my first time with a black man. I loved every inch of him!

—*Rochester, Indiana*

AN OUNCE OF PREVENTION
AIDS Risk Reduction Guidelines
for Healthier Sex
As Recommended by New York Physicians for Human Rights

1. Know your partner, his state of health, his lifestyle and how many different sexual partners he has. If you enjoy being with a partner, see him again. The fewer different partners, the less your risk of acquiring a disease.

2. Engage in sex in a setting which is conducive to good hygiene. Be certain to wash any part of the body contacting the rectal area before contact with the mouth.

3. Both partners should shower together as part of foreplay to check for sores, lymph glands, etc. which might not have been noticed by the other partner.

4. Kissing, cuddling, massaging and mutual masturbation have a very low risk of transmitting disease.

5. Exchanging certain body fluids has a higher risk of transmitting diseases. Swallowing semen, urine or feces increases your risk of acquiring a sexually transmitted disease. Oral sex when sores or cuts are present within the mouth has a high risk.

6. Rimming has an extremely high risk of transmitting disease except in a totally monogamous couple after examination by their health care provider.

7. Anal intercourse causes tiny tears in the anus through which germs from both partners can enter the body. Use of a water-soluble lubricant helps reduce friction and tears and should be used even with a condom. Wearing a condom may reduce the risk of transmitting diseases between partners. Anal douching before or after sex increases the risk of acquiring an infection because it removes normal barriers to infections.

8. Fisting is extremely dangerous no matter what precautions are taken.

9. Urinating after sex may reduce your risk of acquiring some infections.

10. Reduce or eliminate the use of all street drugs, alcohol and marijuana, as studies have shown these may impair the body's immune system and your judgment.

11. Maintain your body's immune system by eating well, exercising and getting adequate rest. Cope with stress by learning relaxation techniques (yoga, self-hypnosis etc.). See your physician on a regular schedule to be checked for inapparent diseases.

Sex is an important part of our lives. We owe it to ourselves and to our partners to keep it as healthy (low risk) as we can.

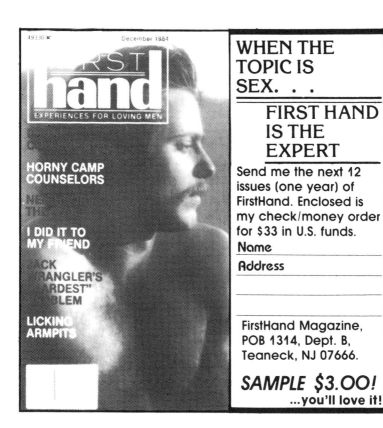

BOOKS FROM GAY SUNSHINE

- [ ] **MEAT/FLESH/SEX/CUM/JUICE/WADS.** Best selling True Homosexual Experiences from S.T.H. Ed. by Boyd McDonald. Volumes 1–6. $13.00 each postpaid (or $73 for all six)
- [ ] **HOT ACTS/ORGASMS: HOMOSEXUAL ENCOUNTERS FROM FIRST HAND** Volumes 1 and 2. $11 each
- [ ] **LUST (Licentious Underground Sexy True Gay Experiences).** True gay experiences $10.95
- [ ] **TRASH: True Revelations and Strange Happenings from 18 Wheeler.** Sexual encounters with truckers. Ed. by John Dagion $12.00
- [ ] **SURFER SEX** Gay Encounters from Australia, by Rusty Winter. $8.95
- [ ] **MY BROTHER MY LOVER** A novel by Tim Barrus $8.95
- [ ] **BEHOLD A PALE HORSE** A novel of homosexuals under the Nazi tyranny by Lannon D. Reed. $11.00
- [ ] **MANSEX** Leather short fiction by Max Exander $9.95
- [ ] **BAYOU BOY** & other stories from Texas by Lars Eighner $8.95
- [ ] **UNZIPPED/DREAM STUD:** Two Collections of short fiction by John Coriolan $8.95 each ($17 for both)
- [ ] **THE GREAT AMERICAN GAY PORNO NOVEL** by Mike Shearer. Sexual adventures of several all-American boys. $10.00
- [ ] **CORPORAL IN CHARGE OF TAKING CARE OF CAPTAIN O'MALLEY.** Erotic short fiction by Jack Fritscher $11.00
- [ ] **SEX BEHIND BARS** by Robert Boyd. Prison stories. $11.00
- [ ] **BLACK MEN/WHITE MEN** Fiction/sexual accounts/photos. $10.00
- [ ] **URBAN ABORIGINALS** by Geoff Mains. Leathersexuality. $10.00
- [ ] **PRETTY BOY DEAD** Gay mystery novel (Joseph Hansen) $10.00
- [ ] **FACING IT** A Novel of AIDS by Paul Reed $8.95

TO ORDER: Check books wanted & send check/money order to G.S. Press, P.O. Box 40397 San Francisco, CA 94140. **Postage included in prices quoted.** (Calif. residents add 6% sales tax.) Mailed in unmarked book envelopes. Add $1 for complete illustrated catalogue.

Published in paperback
There is also a special edition of ten numbered copies,
handbound in boards